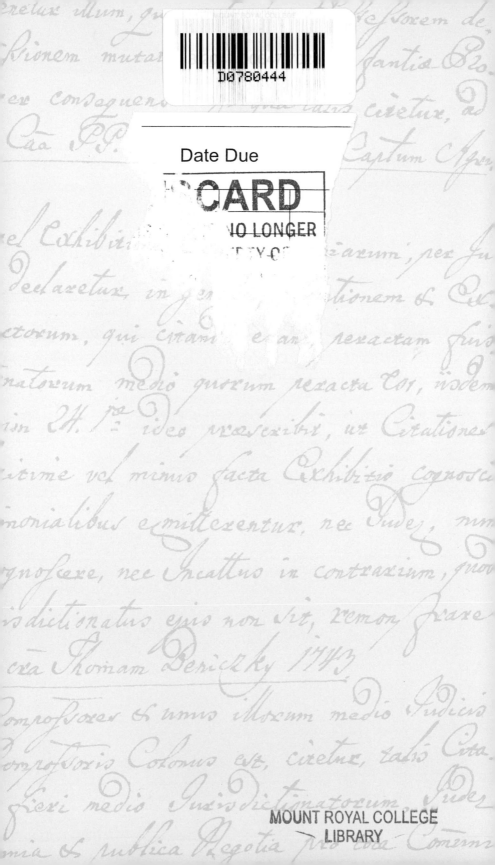

Trading in
MEMORIES

Trading in

MEMORIES

❧❧

Travels Through a Scavenger's
Favorite Places

BARBARA HODGSON

GREYSTONE BOOKS
Douglas & McIntyre Publishing Group
Vancouver/Toronto/Berkeley

Greystone Books
A division of Douglas & McIntyre Ltd.
2323 Quebec Street, Suite 201
Vancouver, British Columbia
Canada v5T 4S7
www.greystonebooks.com

LIBRARY AND ARCHIVES CANADA CATALOGUING IN PUBLICATION

Hodgson, Barbara, 1955–
    Trading in memories : travels through a scavenger's
favorite places / Barbara Hodgson

Includes bibliographical references and index.
ISBN 978-1-55365-199-4

    1. Material culture—History. I. Title
HF5482.H63 2007   306.4'609   C2006-906329-x

Editing by Nancy Flight
Copyediting by Mary Schendlinger
Jacket and book design by Barbara Hodgson/Byzantium Books
Printed and bound in China by C&C Offset Printing Co. Ltd.
Printed on acid-free paper
Distributed in the U.S. by Publishers Group West

We gratefully acknowledge the financial support of the Canada Council for the Arts, the British Columbia Arts Council, and the Government of Canada through the Book Publishing Industry Development Program (BPIDP) for our publishing activities.

All uncredited images are from Byzantium Archives. Images without attribution are from unknown sources or by unknown artists. Every effort has been made to trace accurate ownership of copyrighted text and visual material used in this book. Errors or omissions will be corrected in subsequent editions, provided notification is sent to the publisher.

Contents

A market in Italy, 1908.

Travels in Bric-a-Brac

IN 1985, THE MAXIMUM CUSTOMS ALLOWANCE PERMITTED TO Canadians returning from outside the country was three hundred dollars. Even then it was a paltry amount, and most people lied to remain below it, not so much to save the duty as to avoid the Byzantine paperwork. In October of that year, following a month-long trip to Greece, my customs declaration amounted to sixty-five dollars, and I was truthfully reporting everything. Most of the items in my backpack were scraps of paper picked up off the street: tobacco tax stamps, posters, letters, programs for musical recitals. The most extravagant item was a find from the Piraeus flea market: the lid to a can, wrapped with paper on which was printed a lurid picture of a woman playing the bouzouki. It cost three dollars.

To this day, the bouzouki lady and the torn pieces of paper, still coated with dust and imprinted with treads from a variety of shoes, bring back memories of that stay in Greece more clearly than any purchased souvenir could. I sift through my treasures and remember that it was an enchanting and uneventful trip—the way good trips are—to places on the beaten track, Naxos, Paros, Sifnos, where I did little but walk along hot thyme- and juniper-scented trails, or swim in the clear, invigorating Aegean, afterward letting the seawater dry into a salty, prickly second skin. The pleasures were tangible and intense and, thanks to my bits of detritus, instantly recallable.

There are many ways of seeing and appreciating where you are at any given moment. Visiting museums and monuments may be one person's goal; for another, it is meeting people or climbing mountains. For me, it is collecting fragments of people's material lives: advertisements of rooms for rent, pleas for the return of lost dogs, and announcements of saints' days; bundles of family letters,

photograph negatives, and bills; old books with inscribed flyleaves or curious notes left between the pages.

This search for memories takes me down streets and alleys, through immense, ostentatious cemeteries and tiny, obscure museums dedicated to idiosyncratic personalities or endeavors, and into book-stores, antique shops, and flea markets around the world. These places are where a city's distinct personality can come to life, at times overwhelmingly so. Always there is an odor: the dust and petrol of the street, the cut-flower offerings of the graveyard, the mothballs of the antique store, and, at the markets, the stink of masses of bodies, mixing with—depending on the locale—red wine, coffee, hot dogs, or roasted chickens, for this is a hungry business. And everywhere there is noise—perhaps a hushed turning of pages or a muted discussion, more likely strident shouts, loud music, blaring horns.

It is in the streets, the bookstores, and the markets where a city tantalizingly and coyly reveals its most intimate self, displaying the contents of its attics and trash bins. What can we tell of a place from these once-private possessions, now displayed, discarded, or for sale? This is the question that I address in this ramble through cities from Brussels to Istanbul to Los Angeles.

Choosing which cities to include was far from easy. Why pick Brussels over Amsterdam? Why Naples and not Rome? What is there about Los Angeles that made me choose it over New York? The answer is elusive and perhaps not very sensible: I have focused on those places where I found the greatest pleasure and the most revealing loot.

I have no use for shops where every image is sequestered in a gilt frame, where every scrap has been examined for its monetary value; I'm not understood at those places. The streets and the anarchic markets that resemble my brain—that's where I go. There I find stacks of tattered prints stowed in moldy, claustrophobic cellars that reek of foxing. Grime coats my fingers; my hands become dry and friable like the brittle papers they devour. I find books so thick and warm and textured that I want to lie down and sleep between the pages. I savor the taste of age and leave with threads from torn bindings clinging to my hair.

Portfolios filled with photographs in a Paris bookshop.

Scouring a city for its material secrets is an occupation for an indefatigable and weatherproof walker. Rain or shine, on any given weekend, in almost any city—in gyms, arenas, parking lots, garages—it seems that everything anybody has ever owned is up for sale or trade. Expectations of place are turned upside down, and whole new cities are revealed, as the stories behind the objects and those selling them are considered. French expatriates fleeing Shanghai in 1937–38, for example, left behind chandeliers, dishes, and handbags that now appear among the traditional jade and lacquer ware at that city's Dongtai market. Eastern European immigrants to Canada in the 1920s and '30s brought with them photographs and documents, their only tie to their distant homeland. These people have passed away now, and their memories inevitably end up at garage sales across the West. Postcards, glass lantern slides, stereoscope cards, and family albums from around the world attest to the restlessness of everyone just about everywhere.

My own treasures are papers, books, and photographs with a potent ability to evoke time and place. A worm-holed Arabic document recalls the aroma of burning olive wood filling the nights in Marrakech; a creased and faded photograph of a temple reminds me—through a convoluted path of associations—of swimming among sunbeams and marble columns in the baths of Budapest.

Why collect old stuff, things that are no longer functional or relevant? Why buy a Bakelite telephone with a rotary dial now, when every call you make requires a push of buttons on a touch-tone pad? Why rescue a dusty, disintegrating velvet hat crowned with an ostrich feather that will only attract more dust because you haven't room to display it properly?

It is not necessary to acquire even a single thing to take pleasure in the wealth of the past. For the unattainable—a cemetery statue, for instance—a sketch or a photo must suffice. As for items within reach, some of my strongest memories come from things that I passed up. Like the fisherman describing the proverbial fish that got away, I have magnified the value or beauty of these scorned items. What caused me to reject them? As everyone who has ever plunged into the world of markets and antiques knows, if you don't buy something you think you want or need when you see it, you will *never* have another chance. I have excuses ready, but they seem feeble now.

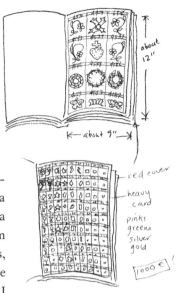

Seen at Porte de Vanves

about 12"

←— about 9" —→

red cover

heavy card

pinks greens silver gold

1000 €!

Topping the list of my regrets is the salesman's sample book from France containing notions for uniforms, vestments, and dresses, dated about 1880. Its stiff pages were thick with braids, buttons, frogs, laurel wreaths, crowns of thorns, votive hearts, and medallions in metals, silken threads, and semiprecious stones of the deepest reds, the richest golds, and the most glittery silvers. With a crow-quill pen, a clerk had painstakingly drawn a grid to separate each sample and had labeled them with now-faded numbers. Generals, cardinals, and aristocratic ladies and gentlemen were adorned from catalogs such as this one, and I decided against it because it was far too expensive. But remembering it gives me a great deal of pleasure. It was something I had never dreamed existed.

What drives people into this kind of trade? There is no doubt that acquisition—or, to use a gentler word, accumulation—is at the heart of it. Is there something more? Perhaps the sense that by touching, seeing, and smelling the past, you've got some small claim on it.

The hunt for castoffs is a quiet, peaceful occupation in spite of the disorderly chaos surrounding it. There's a lazy decadence to looking through to the past that cannot be measured by clocks, or by current standards of perfection. Everything I have is flawed in some way or another: a series is incomplete, a spine is frayed, water or fire has wreaked its damage. At times I sigh and vow that I will make this rat's nest worth something. Or perhaps I'll leave it just as it is, for I've learned over the years that there is beauty not only in perfection but also in erosion, possession, and remembrance. Any object that has been owned and then discarded is welcome if only for the fleeting traces of its past reflected on its surface. Its history will become part of a new story; its gift is authority and authenticity.

B.L.   Maps.
69810(18) America! Hieronymus Cock after
     Diego Gutiérrez, Antwerp 1562 Copperplate e[...]
     "Americae sive quartae orbis partis nova
     descriptio..." "One of 2 earlest known
     surviving printed wall maps

     shows mermaids & the giant Patagonians

Annotated map   → handwriting all along the
                          margin

MAGNA CARTA

East India Archives housed at B.L.
Cpt Francis Stains Log Book (1711) is
quite interesting

Lindisfarne
Gospels
c.698

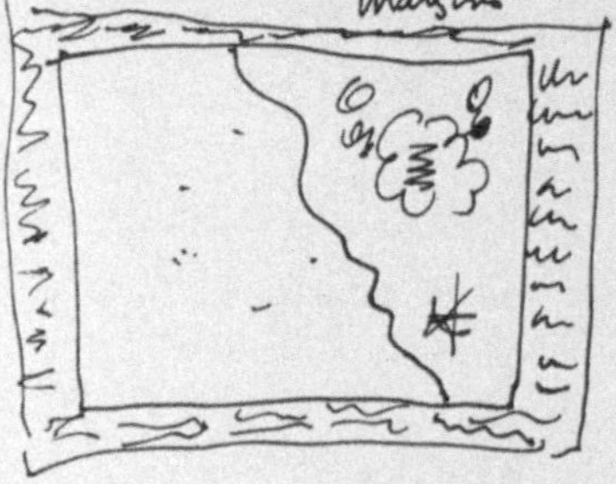

The travels of Si[r]
Mandeville
-Bohemia, begin[s]
15th c.
[Add. MS 24189,

28 miniatures pa[...]
Bohemia used [...]
tech of semi-g[...]
(?) on vellum w[...]
has been tinted gree[n]
- All drawings rela[...]
the travels but the[...]
no text in this vo[...]

Thomas Bird Mosh[...]
"The Pirate Princ[e]
Publishing" Brit[...]
Catalogue of the
hundreds of book[s]
(inc those of Bust[...]
that he published
permission

Gutenberg Bible 1454-5

British Film Inst. Movie list
BFI Stills, Posters & Designs
21 Stephen St. London W1P2LN
Tel - 44-(0)171 255-1444
Fax   436-7950

Wellcome
bottle 
← stainless steel
bottle top

← clear, thickish
glass.

rag stuffed
inside

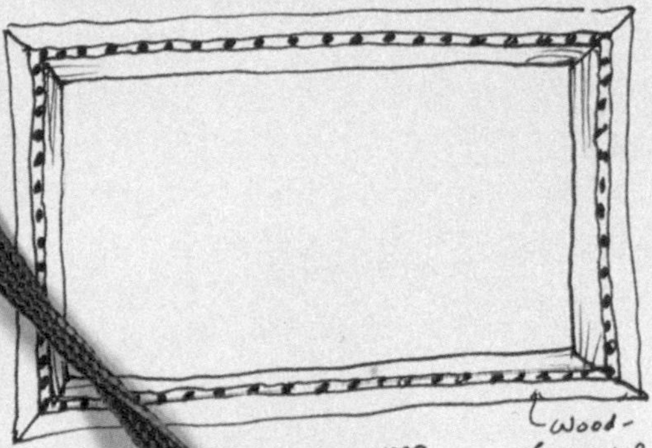

Hippolyte uses as specimen
reliquary boxes w/o concerning himself
boxes w/o concerning himself
about their real intended use.

Hippolyte stamps every
page, signs it and leaves
space for Marie to write
her approval.

He also pastes
down all kinds of
correct---

different
heights?

Wood-
(or metal)
little metal
bit stuck
in depression
could work as a
specimen box

filigree metal
heart case
with a
pad inside.
This could
be interesting
if it wasn't
a heart.
about 1/4"
thick
about
120%.
size shown

Specimen Box

Too many boxes

Angels

ALTHOUGH BROMPTON CEMETERY IN EARL'S COURT is considered one of London's grand graveyards, it is actually quite modest. Well kept, not too tightly packed, it is frequented (at least during daylight) by the kind of people who take brisk walks through parks. There are few names of note within, and the place is seldom mentioned in guidebooks.

Located in southwest London, Brompton was established in 1836, one of seven privately run facilities that included Kensal Green and Highgate. The opening of these commercial cemeteries in the 1830s was permitted by an act of Parliament to help cope with the growing numbers of dead, the result of a rapidly increasing population that was succumbing to rampant disease.

I first went there to pass some time while waiting for the Earl's Court Youth Hostel to open its doors for the evening. I meandered up and down the lanes and dutifully read the headstones—the "Rest in peace's," the "Sorrowfully missed's"—and wondered, when I noticed long lists of names on single tombs, if it was economy or affection that drove certain families to crowd in together.

Not being a cemetery aficionado at the time, I ignored a lot of detail—including the replica of St Peter's Basilica—but I did notice the impressive quantity of granite and marble statues. The cemetery seemed to be a parking lot for angels.

ABOVE: *Cherubim console one who died young.*

FACING PAGE: *An angel in waiting at a London cemetery.*

PREVIOUS SPREAD: *Notes made in London, during a visit to the British Library.*

I would have forgotten my dawdle except for one thing: a tiny two-word notice, lettered in brass at the corner of one gravestone, nearly at ground level and almost obscured by grass. It read "North Exit."

My first thought was that it was a nifty piece of recycling. Or perhaps it was a joke; then I decided that it was just plain bizarre. Since then, I have made a point of visiting graveyards wherever I go, looking

THE LANGUAGE OF
VICTORIAN CEMETERIES
Some common and
mystifying tombstone
symbols:
Anchor: a disguised cross
Broken column: an
untimely death
Keys: alone, a symbol of
spiritual knowledge;
in the hands of an
angel, the means of
entering heaven
Lamp: spiritual
knowledge
Lion: a guard against
evil
Palm: eternal peace,
among others
Pyramid: eternity;
protection against
Satan's resting on
the grave
Swords, crossed: death
in battle
Snake swallowing its own
tail: eternity
Thistle: sorrow on earth
Urn: mourning, the urn
being the body for the
soul, often shown
draped
Wheat: resurrection

for oddities. No matter what one considers odd—aged ladies spending their pensions to feed churchyard cats, memento mori constructed of soccer balls, or eternal flames flickering in 7-Up bottles—it is certain to be found in some cemetery somewhere. In Paris *cimetières,* signs are erected to remind inhabitants that their time in subterranean Paris is limited: that if their graves are not kept up, they will be evicted. In Naples, the caretakers of the *cimiteri* harangue sightseers to put away their cameras, draping an *omerta,* so to speak, over the already silenced dead. In Athens, bones of the disinterred are set out to dry in the hot, revivifying Greek sun. In Vancouver, a majestic columbarium is filled with the ashes of expatriate Italians; their photographic portraits stare out from flower-laden niches.

London remains one of my favorite cemetery cities, for it is in London that the very British longing to be dead as flamboyantly as alive reaches its zenith. And, in spite of the British inclination to reside elsewhere, a good many expatriates have returned to London to die. Richard and Isabel Burton's Bedouin tent tomb at Mortlake (on the outskirts of London) gives them the best of both their native and their adopted lands. Representatives of the whole world have come to London, expired, then helped themselves to indefinite hospitality. One of the most famous of them, Karl Marx, slumbers in Highgate, under a massive portrait bust that is impossible to disregard. In spite of the celebrities to be found, London cemeteries are largely dismissed by seekers of the famous, as most of the really big names are interred in churches such as Westminster Abbey.

Highgate, once called the North London Cemetery, is admired for its architecture and its relatively dense selection of celebrity inhabitants. It has long been

established on the tourist map; hours are limited, admission is charged, and photography is restricted. Joining a tour is the only way to see the older and—with its Egyptian-style avenue and catacombs—more distinctive Western half. It opened in 1839 and contains the chemical genius Michael Faraday, as well as three of the Rossettis—Gabriele, Christina, and Elizabeth Siddal, the wife of the poet Dante Gabriel Rossetti. When Elizabeth died of an overdose of laudanum, Dante Gabriel, carried away with grief, buried a manuscript of his poems along with her. Seven years later, regretting his emotional gesture, he had her body exhumed in the dead of night and retrieved the poems. Her state of preservation, which was apparently almost perfect, must have rattled him to the core. Afterward, he refused to be buried in the same place and so now rests in Birchington-on-Sea, where he died in 1882.

An Egyptian temple at Kensal Green Cemetery.

Judiciously minimal maintenance keeps the Western section in a state of Gothic eeriness, and there is nothing like visiting on a drizzly day in early spring or late fall, when few others are inclined to join the tour. Absolute loneliness, rainwater dripping from the mossy branches of the trees, and the unrelenting grayness of the sky and the monuments, unrelieved by fresh foliage or bright flowers, are perfect conditions for conjuring up a few ghosts. Parts of the newer Eastern section also have a lovely overgrown feel, despite the new tenants that are still accepted there.

Kensal Green, established in northwest London in 1832, is a pleasant contrast to the fame of Highgate. Baedeker's 1908 guidebook singles out the four inhabitants of the more prominent tombs: Andrew Ducrow, the circus rider; G.H. Robins, the auctioneer; James Morison, the pill maker; and John St John Long, the Quack. How did Baedeker overlook Arctic explorer John Ross, Constantinople visitor Julia Pardoe, globetrotter Lady Jane Franklin, or the incomparable Emile Blondin, who inched across Niagara Falls on a tightrope?

For seekers of scandal, there is Baronne de Feuchères, née Sophie Dawes (1795–1840), the daughter of a fisherman. Onetime mistress of the Duc de Bourbon, and estranged wife of the Baron de Feuchères, Sophie was accused of murdering her husband after he was found hanging from a curtain rod in his bedroom. His death was determined to be suicide; nevertheless, his estate became hopelessly entangled, as would-be heirs tried to prevent Sophie from collecting any benefits from his death.

Although Kensal Green has its true celebrities—Wilkie Collins, Anthony Trollope, and William Makepeace Thackeray are three whose graves I missed—few people aside from mourners or joggers go there, except on weekends, when tours are offered. The light attendance could be the fault of the tube ride, if ours was typical. A group of young men brandishing sixteen-ounce cans of beer got on at the Queen's Park stop and proceeded to raise hell, yelling and gesturing lewdly. The next stop was Kensal Green, where we mercifully escaped. Several people changed cars there; the passengers who remained with the sodden louts must have been comatose, or perhaps they enjoyed the boisterous, obscene antics. It is a long walk from the station to the cemetery along Harrow Road. What can be seen of the cemetery grounds through the fence is discouraging, as the view is mainly of weeds.

These souvenir offerings at Kensal Green—not to everyone's taste—owe their existence to its neglect: litter along certain paths turned out to be shards of blue-and-white pottery, and huge patches of weeds provided specimens for pressing.

Those who are not pursuing a Burke-and-Hare grave-robbing career, who are kind enough to leave hands and heads on the statues, and who would never steal

KENSAL GREEN CEMETARY
MAY 16

wreaths, will find that souvenir hunting in a cemetery has its limita-
tions. Anyone with a camera, however, will be content to spend
hours, if not days, photographing the immobile and uncomplaining
angels.

The angels' poses and expressions are myriad, a veritable glossary
of Victorian morbidness. There are angels guarding spirits, carrying
away souls, mourning an untimely end, slumbering in sympathy,
weeping, and making offerings. They are frequently shown with one
or both arms outstretched, pleading for mercy or pointing the way to
heaven. Most have wings; some also have halos or crowns.

All levels of angeldom are represented, including the six-winged
seraphim with their flaming swords, and two-winged cherubim,
usually naked except for a cloth about the middle and a pair of shoes,
holding out an open book, a symbol of faith. Thrones, pursuing
justice, often carry scales; dominions are crowned and proffer staffs;
virtues typically hold lilies or roses; powers wear the armor of
knights and may carry a sword or lead a chained demon; principalities
are robed over their soldier's gear; and both archangels and angels
appear as soldiers.

In addition to these angels, there are lambs (representing Christ
and found on children's graves), skulls (a sign of mortality), poppies
(for eternal sleep), and an eye within a triangle (the all-seeing eye of
God). Then there is the architecture. Tombs in cemeteries from
London to Cairo to Punta Arenas have been constructed in most of
the major building styles, and it is possible to find small-scale
Egyptian temples, obelisks, Gothic chapels, Greek pantheons,
Japanese pagodas, Art Deco *maisons*, and, as already mentioned,
Bedouin tents, to name but a few.

The cemetery experience
is not complete until you
take the tube to the Angel
station and consider the
old wills and probates on
offer at the Camden
Passage antique market
(see next page).

Rare are the places where the ordinary person can
get close to a statue without being chastised or
charged a fee. At most cemeteries, as long as you treat
the monuments respectfully (this means not climbing
up on them or interrupting funerals), you are free to
get as close as you wish. If nothing else, such proximity
gives you a chance to revel in your own graveless
state.

+

Bank Bg
At 15 746

Probate

Of the will and codicil of

M.ʳ William Hayley Englehart

Severns

Legal Heirs

Extracted by Dyke & Stokes
Proctors Doctors Commons

110
33
4 2

✓ 230 23

Angel

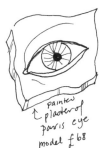

painted
plaster of
paris eye
model £68

A PORTAL TO ONE OF LONDON'S SMALLER but more interesting antique markets, Camden Passage, is an angel of another sort, the rather uncelestial tube station at Islington.

In the seventeenth century, Islington was in the country. Like other pleasant nearby towns, it became a refuge for well-heeled Londoners, desperately fleeing first the plague and then the Great Fire. It became a suburb in the following century, but development and industry invaded in the nineteenth century and it deteriorated into slums. Its gentrification, begun after World War II, is well in hand.

The Angel station is located at the Angel, the confluence of St John Street and Goswell, Pentonville, and City roads. This intersection was named after an old coaching tavern that had long been established in the area.

Camden Passage, a short walk from the Angel, is the destination of most tourists to Islington. It is a tranquil passageway once known as Cumberland Row and renamed in 1876 after the Earl of Camden, Charles Pratt, a chief justice. It was officially opened as an antique-store passage in September 1960. The narrow lane has the feel of a village high street. It is lined with small, low buildings made of natural or whitewashed brick, featuring doors and windows painted with the heavy, glossy enamel that characterizes Britain's domestic architecture.

During most weekdays, antique and print dealers operate out of storefronts along this lane. The stores are more or less permanent, but the trade is unreliable, so turnover can be high and hours are haphazard. Indeed, restaurants threaten to take the area over entirely.

A stall at one of London's many markets. Luggage and taxidermy are popular items.

One longtime dealer—a stout man with luxuriously shaggy eyebrows—at the entrance to the passage, stocks old playing cards and is a font of information about the history of games. Another, who closed down a few years ago, had bins full of one-pound prints from early-1800s editions of the *Encyclopædia Britannica* and *Encyclopædia Londinensis.* He sold these alongside Albinus engravings that flaunted fourteen-hundred-pound price tags.

Camden Passage was also the site of a small Thursday morning book fair. At my last visit, in the late 1990s, one stall was still operating. The books were mostly cheap paperbacks, but a box labeled "miscellaneous" held some interest for the ephemera hunter. A sample of its offerings: a booklet promoting electricity, a receipt for a walking stick, and montages made up of dozens of tiny Victorian photographs of ladies, gentlemen, and dogs.

More consistent are the outdoor antique markets, held from seven until two on Wednesdays and from eight until four on Saturdays. These markets, like the shops, are subject to the vagaries of economics, but on good days, when there is a full complement of stall holders, stuff is heaped along the lane, tucked into odd corners, and piled up sets of stairs, finally spilling into a small plaza. The objects range from demolition plunder—incomplete doorknobs and knockers, chandelier bits, faucets, and window latches—to finer pieces, including leather luggage and mahogany boxes. Walking sticks, dolls, paint boxes, medicine bottles, and prints are plentiful. Opening onto this plaza are a couple of tiny arcades,

each with vendors specializing in some collectible or other. Militaria, Greek and Roman artifacts, paintings, and crystal are a few that I've noticed.

And what about angels? It has suddenly occurred to me that among all the prints and objects I've acquired from Camden Passage, on the subjects of minerals, botany, ornithology, engineering, pyrotechnics, esoteric rituals, the arts, naval history, and travel, I haven't found a single angel.

Jeu de Balle

ALTHOUGH BRUSSELS IS NOT A LARGE CITY, IT HAS a disorienting layout with no respect for grid or planning. The map on the facing page, although printed in 1910, accurately represents Brussels's unpredictable cartography. Only rue de Fiennes runs east–west, and it leads nowhere of consequence for the visitor. No street runs north–south. The myriad curves, angles, *places*, and *passages* twist newly arrived pedestrians off course and lead them miles in the wrong direction. It was thus when I first went to the Jeu de Balle flea market in the working-class Marolles district not far from the Gare du Midi, Brussels's main train station. According to the map, the market was close to my hotel, but I took several wrong turns and so added some distance to what should have been a brief stroll.

I must have been distracted by the cobblestone streets and lovely stone buildings in various stages of disrepair or redevelopment. Having been established in the twelfth century and developed in spurts, the Marolles exhibits a little bit of every style, from Romanesque to baroque, from neoclassical to twentieth-century muddle. The homey touches—lace curtains, scrubbed doorsteps, personalized nameplates, and windowsill ornaments—made me envy the tenants of even the shabbiest of these buildings.

FACING PAGE: *Bruxelles. From* Belgium and Holland *(Leipzig: Karl Baedeker, 1910).*

PREVIOUS SPREAD: *Finds from the Jeu de Balle flea market, including Le Nain jaune.*

I stopped occasionally to photograph posters and painted mailboxes and to consult the map, which became more confusing the farther I went. As pages from old schoolbooks fluttered by, however, I sensed that I was getting near. I gathered them up, certain that they were a signal, like candy dropped to entice Hansel and Gretel.

The scattered pages did finally lead, in a circuitous way, to the flea market, but it was apparent from the

protected aspect of the square that they could not have come from there. Examining them later, I realized that they weren't so old after all. Some frustrated child had simply torn them out of her book.

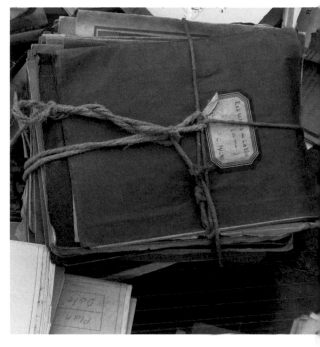

There is no lack of torn-up schoolbooks, or any other sort of book or periodical or magazine, at the Marché de la place du Jeu de Balle, established in 1873 and open for business every day of the week since 1919. According to Les Amis du vieux marché (The Friends of the Old Market), there are 450 stalls. Each of them contributes to the impression that the square is chockablock with boxes overfilled with paper. It is no use going to the Jeu de Balle to find something specific; there is no organization, no theme—only great heaps of stuff.

But there is more than just paper. There are microscope slides, 78s, pressed plants, watch parts, unfashionable jackets, dysfunctional violins, cracked crockery, down-at-the-heel shoes, and, above all, objects that have lost their identity. Jeu de Balle bursts with the useless and the ugly. It is a *vide-grenier* ("empty the attic") in the truest sense of the word.

When I first dove into this mess, I had the sense of what it must be like to be a rag picker or a dumpster diver. Or a member of a massive flock of crows, settling down to a nice scavenge in some insalubrious field. I thought about the travails of making a living hauling boxes out of cellars into trucks; then, in the darkness of the early morning, out of trucks onto squares like Jeu de Balle; then, at the end of the day, back into trucks to go—where? Back to the

market the next day and the day after that until their contents are so
weatherworn and picked over that finally they have nowhere to go
but the dump? Or to be left on the spot for the truly desperate to
scavenge? A French friend introduced me to the word *transbahutage*,
the constant shifting of stuff.

Transbahutage at least has the benefit of movement and planning.
It is the *attente*, the long hours of standing around waiting to make a
sale, all year round, in the dark, the cold, the blazing sun, the rain,
that would grind most people down. It is no wonder that the vendors
have a strong confraternity, especially obvious in the boisterous
exchanges of good-natured insults that wipe out any shreds of
rivalry and give a raw joy to the whole business. It may not be pretty,
but a morning spent in this kind of company makes Brussels's other
famous market, Les Antiquaires de la place du Sablon, seem wan and
lifeless in comparison.

Little imagination is needed to transport the visitor back to 1873,
Jeu de Balle's opening year. Secondhand goods had been sold at markets in Brussels since at least the 1500s, so the tradition was already
well established. The merchandise was brought in carts pulled by
horses, donkeys, men, women. Instead of spreading goods out on
plastic tarps or in cardboard boxes, the merchants displayed their
wares on the bare cobblestones, rough hemp cloths, wicker baskets,
or trestle tables. Many sold directly off the backs of their carts.

Rags, old clothing, wool, and sewing notions were the main
goods for sale; paper and photographs were rare commodities.
Frames, amateur oil paintings, vases, candlesticks, dinnerware, and
cutlery were plentiful. Then, as now, the cafés and restaurants surrounding the square did a brisk business, serving up beer, red wine,
and *moules frites*.

The vendors then were Belgians, with the occasional Dutch or
French interloper. Today they are a mix of Belgians of both French
and Flemish origins, sub-Saharan Africans, and Moroccans. If
there are other ethnic types in the mix, they must learn to yell
louder or remain forever unrecognized. The Belgians aspire to
become antiquarians, and the Africans offer folk art and musical
instruments. The Moroccans sell whatever comes to hand. They are

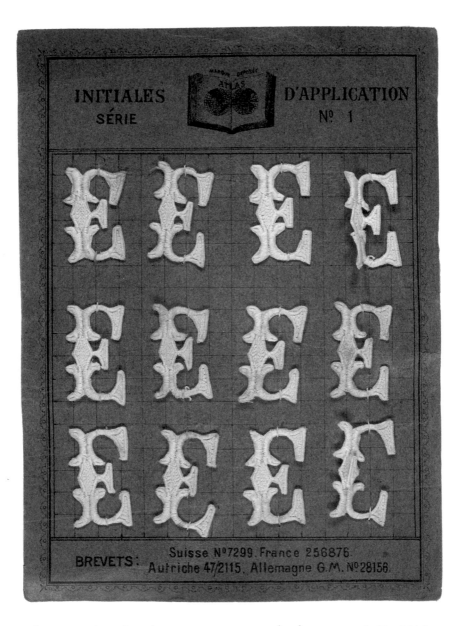

INITIALES SÉRIE

MARQUE DÉPOSÉE
ATLAS

D'APPLICATION
N°. 1

BREVETS: Suisse N°7299. France 256876.
Autriche 47/2115. Allemagne G.M. N°28156.

the ones who advertise to carry away trash, then
resell what they think is too good to throw away,
which is almost everything. In most cases, it is
doubtful that any thought has been given to worthiness; that is for
the buyer to decide.

A card of lace initial Es.
Cost: one euro.

Overall, French is the lingua franca, with Flemish and *brusseleer*,
the local French-based dialect, audible beneath the surface, but the
Maghrebian Arabic is more insistent, more apparent. I asked one

Moroccan, with whom I bargained for a watercolor paint box by expressing interest in his selection of pious cards of Sainte-Marie, if he missed his country. He told me that he and his friends were dreadfully homesick. "We miss the sun," he said, "and the other beautiful things of the Mediterranean, the olive and orange trees, especially. Our language," he added, "is the one thing that keeps our home alive."

During several visits in 2004, found treasures included colorful boards of the traditional game Le Nain jaune (literally, "yellow dwarf"), probably of relatively recent manufacture but of a style that has not changed since before World War II, though the game itself dates back to the late eighteenth century. I also found sturdy, slim boxes that once carried Lumière-brand glass photographic plates, X-rays of the hands of a Monsieur Valentine, and unexposed pre-1960s photographic printing paper, precious not only because it is almost impossible to find in usable condition but also because it is single weight with a lovely matte finish. When one vendor asked ten euros for his box of paper, I declined, but the price dropped by half on the next pass by. Another dealer, unaware of what he had, asked twenty euros for a similar item, just in case it was something valuable. When I shook my head, he proceeded to undo the pristine wrappers to see what was in the box, thus exposing the paper and rendering it absolutely unusable.

A stout, red-faced Flemish woman with the harsh voice of a newspaper boy sold delicate laces. Squeezed into a quilted jacket, her hair more or less pulled back in a bun, her stubby fingers adept at pocketing coins, she could have been one of the original vendors of the 1870s. Her repeated "un euro" shot out across the square like cannon fire. No mean feat at a place where many voices compete.

In 2005, when I visited again, the haphazardness of the trade had replaced the photography supplies and games with taxidermy, crusty bottles of dubious wine, and ever more boxes of the bills, envelopes, and letters that cram attics around the world. The lace lady, however, was not to be seen—or heard.

A find from the Jeu de Balle: X-rays of the hand of Monsieur Valentine, 1965. Cost: half a euro.

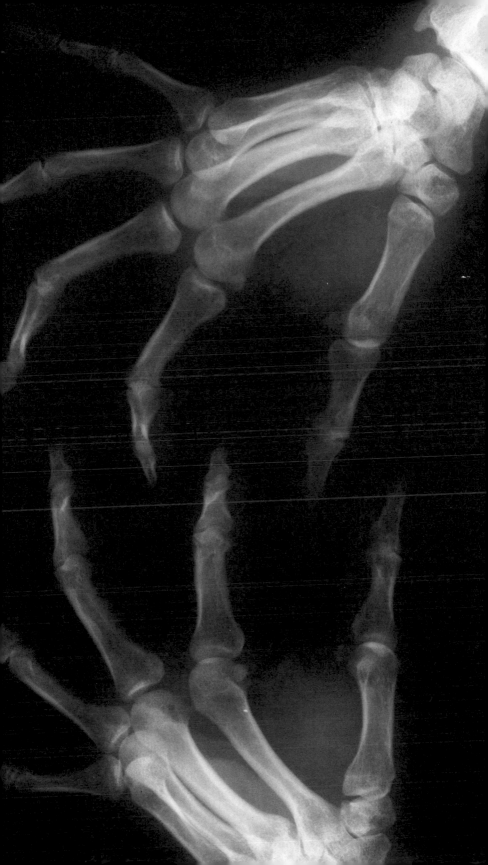

Les Puces

CONSIDER THIS MOMENT OF INDEFINABLE pleasure, a momentary step into the past. Returning to my Paris hotel from *les puces,* the flea market, at the Porte de Vanves, I hear, "Madame, you've dropped something!" I turn around and walk back to the man who has called out. He is holding the newspaper I had bought from a secondhand paper dealer. He unrolls it—he wants to read the latest news—and is overcome by confusion. "Madame"—he is unsure of himself—"this paper is dated 1949." And so it is. I want to ask him what year he thinks we're in, the two of us, strangers, brought together for this brief moment. Why couldn't it be 1949? I wonder how old he was then and guess that, like me, he hadn't even been born. Neither of us could evoke a personal 1949, but by holding that paper we could pretend.

I drop many things. I have left a trail of dollars, pesetas, lire, francs, dinars, and dirhams that crisscrosses North America, Europe, and the Middle East. I have abandoned boarding cards before boarding flights, slept securely on my passport in the beds of dubious hotels only to go out and leave it under the pillow the next morning, left my camera dangling on chair backs in cafés. Perhaps I am drawn to jetsam because I am picking up my own tracks, following myself through city streets, retrieving myself.

Whatever you've lost—yourself, someone else, or a precious object—there are few better places to start looking for it than Paris. With its nine established markets and numerous occasional or impromptu ones, its bookstalls along the Seine, the extraordinary cabinet of curiosities known as Deyrolles on rue de Bac, and

ABOVE: Paris, *a French-language newspaper published in Casablanca in 1949, then bought fifty years later, in Paris.*
FACING PAGE: *A page from an album, c. 1890, showing photos of two Paris markets: Marché aux oiseaux and Foire à la ferraille.*

P A R I S

Marché aux oiseaux. Paris

Foire à la Feraille. Paris boul.d Richard-Lenoir.

the phenomenal auction house Drouot, Paris is one of the great cities of the world for collectors. Those who sell precious or curious objects—and their numbers are legion—have an accumulated sense of the past, an inheritance of knowing what it truly means to trade in memories.

The French writer Honoré de Balzac, shown here on the right, was an especially keen observer of Parisians and their love of castoffs. In his 1848 novel *Cousin Pons* (which, along with *The Wild Ass's Skin*, is required reading for any lover of bric-a-brac), he called Paris "that city in which all the curios in the world manage to come together."[1] Balzac's words are truer than ever today.

In *The Wild Ass's Skin*, he describes how his hero, the young and desperate Raphael de Valentin, is deflected from suicide by a visit to a junk shop on the Quai Voltaire. The owner of the shop is miserly, distrustful, and wily:

ABOVE: *Honoré de Balzac.*

FACING PAGE: *One of Deyrolles's ever-changing and irresistible entrance displays.*

> He seemed to possess the gift of reading thoughts lurking deep in the most secretive of souls. The morality of every nation on the globe, their wisdom too, were summed up on his chilly countenance, just as the products of the entire world were piled up in his dusty showrooms.[2]

On the third floor of the curio dealer's wondrous and claustrophobic cave of Ali Baba, Valentin finds a magical ass's skin that gives him a new lease on life. With it he conjures up prodigious extravagances and is granted the power to thrive on immoral thoughts and wanton behavior. The ass's skin may allow Valentin to command the world's

1 Honoré de Balzac, *Cousin Pons*, 141.
2 Balzac, *The Wild Ass's Skin*, 44.

vices, but it is in the packed corners of the curio shop that we have a foretaste of his cruel fate. For Valentin's imagination takes flight at the sight of "crocodiles, apes and stuffed boas"; wax effigies of medical horrors from the cabinet of Frederik Ruysch, the famous anatomist; mystical altars and tabernacles that hint at profane ceremonies; murderous-looking tomahawks; and enigmatic sarcophagi, no doubt still exuding the stench of their rotting contents. Valentin was convinced that "the ear fancied it heard stifled cries, the mind imagined that it caught the thread of unfinished dramas, and the eye that it perceived half-smothered glimmers."[3]

With the purchase of the wild ass's skin, Valentin's future was assured, and it was every bit as dark and terrible and wondrous as the visions he had while spellbound by the treasures of the curio shop.

Where is today's equivalent of this Quai Voltaire junk shop? Where can we go to astound our imaginations while we hunt for our own talismans? Some would argue that such a place no longer exists; others would insist that it is at the Marché aux puces de Saint-Ouen, a labyrinthine network of markets just beyond the Porte de Clignancourt in the eighteenth arrondissement in north Paris.[4]

With something approaching 2,500 dealers spread out over ten acres, this market is easily the largest in Paris. It is also one of the oldest, having been established by rag dealers shortly after the

Franco-Prussian War of 1870–71. It is made up of some ten separate markets, including the Marchés Jules Vallès, Biron, Dauphine, Michelet, Malassis, Malik, Serpette, Paul Bert, and my favorite, Marché Vernaison, with its scientific instruments, corals, cameras, photographs, telephones, phonographs, stuffed penguin, skulls, and schoolroom anatomical charts, printed on linen in vivid and alarming color.

3 Balzac, *The Wild Ass's Skin*, 35.
4 For the *chineur*, or frequenter of flea markets, a stay in Paris that does not include a weekend is criminal, for though there are markets on every day of the week, of the best ones, the Porte de Vanves is weekends only, and those at the Porte de Clignancourt, though also on Mondays, are busiest on weekends.

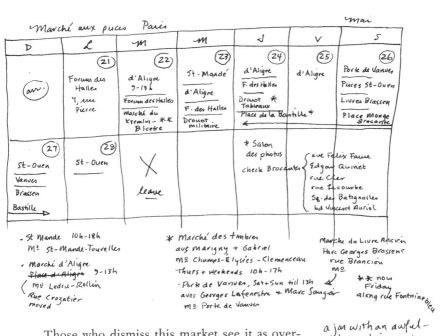

Marché aux puces Paris — mai

D	L	M	M	J	V	S
(am.)	(21) Forum des Halles / 4, rue Pierre	(22) d'Aligre 9-13h / Forum des Halles / Marché du Kremlin - ** Bicêtre	(23) St-Mandé / d'Aligre / F. des Halles / Drouot militaire	(24) d'Aligre / F. des Halles / Drouot Tableaux / Place de la Bastille * ←	(25) d'Aligre	(26) Porte de Vanves / Puces St-Ouen / Livres Brassens / Place Monge Brocante
(27) St-Ouen / Vanves / Brassen / Bastille ▷	(28) St-Ouen	✕ leave		‡ Salon des photos / check Brocantes		(ave Félix Faure / Edgar Quinet / rue Cler / rue Lecourbe / Sq. des Batignolles / bd Vincent Auriol

- St Mandé 10h-18h
  M² St-Mandé-Tourelles
- Marché d'Aligre
  Place d'Aligre 9-13h
  (M² Ledru-Rollin
  Rue Crozatier moved

✱ Marché des timbres
  aux Marigny + Gabriel
  M² Champs-Élysées - Clemenceau
  Thurs + weekends 10h-17h
  · Porte de Vanves, Sat+Sun till 13h
  aves Georges Lefenestre + Marc Sangier
  M² Porte de Vanves

Marché du Livre Ancien
Parc Georges Brassens
rue Brancion
M²
✱✱ now Friday
along rue Fontainebleau

Those who dismiss this market see it as over-priced, touristy, an institution grown tired. Those who love it love the variety, the imperfections, the continuity of a venerable occupation, even if English or German at times seems to swamp the French language (this has always been an international trade).

Imagine, if you will, some of the various stalls at Les Puces Saint-Ouen. Some are disorganized beyond belief. In one of them you might find books stacked high, threatening to topple at the merest breeze; cracked china cups on the shelves, rattling with every passing step; dirt, not dust, coating everything in sight. A stuffed animal is suspended from a beam; cobwebs disguise its identity. Drawers hanging half open are crammed with the detritus of time standing still: broken watches, clocks, gears, springs. The owner of this jumble is one of many

extraordinary types to be found in the flea market, and his goods—all chipped, stained, or no longer functioning—are *his* treasures. He is reluctant to part with any of it: something may come in handy for fixing something else; it may go up in value; he hasn't priced it yet. Who can

a jar with an awful-looking hairy snake

guess his reasons for holding back? In fact, he rarely sells anything and refuses to even talk to anyone he deems unworthy. Questioning him about the origin of any given item only raises his suspicions. For you see, worthiness is not only a question of the value of the object but also of the potential purchaser.

When a coveted object is discovered, the would-be buyer, having recognized the dealer for what he is, hesitates. *"S'il vous plaît, "* are the inevitable first words, *"Combien cela coûte-t-il?"* ("How much is this?") He scowls and reaches out for it. Turning it over and over, as though feeling it will reveal the price, he comes up with something quite absurd. *"Pouvez-vous me faire un prix, s'il vous plaît?"* ("Can you give me a better price, please?") ventures the buyer. He turns away with a look of disgust that says "Take it or leave it," in any language. Reluctantly, the buyer puts the object back exactly where she found it. He rushes over to rearrange it, then gestures with a "Well, what'll you pay?" flick of the hand. She offers something equally absurd. In the rare event that he sells, he will thrust the object at her, unwrapped—or, at best, rolled up in last month's newspaper—and once again turn his back. More likely, he will refuse to even discuss the matter further.

Next door, everything is brightly lit and neatly laid out in convenient clusters, and the cheerful fragrance of potpourri is discernible through the aroma of a lunch of *steak frites* and red wine, which sits alluringly on the cash desk. Prices and descriptions are marked on everything, and some items even show a reduction penned in purple ink, bookended with exclamation marks. *"!!! Vente de soldes!!!* Reduced!! 20% off!! *Remise de 20%!!!"* The dealer—a beautifully coiffured, elegant middle-aged woman wearing silk stockings that cost more than your entire wardrobe—patiently explains what it is, where it came from, how much more it costs elsewhere. The purchase made, the object wrapped in mounds of tissue and securely bagged, a receipt is written out, a credit card is accepted, change is given.

And farther along—as the bargain hunter moves down one of the dozen lanes that make up *les puces*—another merchant, another character. All is neat, well

Marché Vernaison at the Marché aux puces de Saint-Ouen.

lit, and glowing with lemon oil, but there is so much, heaps of textiles, piles of paper, shelves double and triple stacked with crockery and curios, drawers upon drawers of heaven knows what. After some minutes of squeezing through all the stuff, the customer realizes that there is only one option in a place like this: to ask for what one is looking for. The merchant is a friendly sort, perpetually amused by the open mouths of his visitors, but no neophyte when it comes to the trade.

"Ah," he says with a twinkle in his eye, knowing that asking is a step closer to buying, "you are considering something very special, I see." Gradually, as wares are unearthed and spread out, and as the proclaimed values go up accordingly, the buyer begins to stand taller, proudly aware that she has come to resemble the French people she admires so much. She has developed their unique appreciation of precious objects. Her will to negotiate sharpens but is helpless against the inflated prices discussed. Nonetheless, she leaves with what she came for, having somehow happily paid three times her intended limit.

These extremes in merchant types and all those in between are a part of the mystique of the market. Objects retaining even a smidgen of the personality of the dealer are all the more precious for this extra layer of memory. Balzac would certainly approve.

FACING PAGE: *Vintage postcards displayed at a now-defunct Paris postcard shop, 1997.*
FOLLOWING SPREAD: *Notes made in France while searching for Pierre Loti images.*

PUCES

- Marché du kremlin - Bicêtre   M° kremlin - Bicêtre
  Mardi 9 - 18h (actually better around 11h)
  Cartes postales, etc.

- Marché Riquet : M° Riquet
   42, rue Riquet
   Mercredi 9h - 13h et 16h à 18h30

- marché des Collections   . M° Hôtel-de-Ville
   9h à 18h — Vendredi
   Esplanade / gérant l'Hôtel - de - Ville

- Porte de Vanves   M° Porte de Vanves (14e)
  Marc Sagnier et av Georges Lafenestre
  Sat, Sun, 7 - 18h (many give up around 13h)
  7 - 19h ?

✓ Saint-Mandé
  10h - 18h mercredi
  M° St-Mandé-Tourelles
  rue de Paris

Marché d'Aligre   mardi-
                   vendredi
Place d'Aligre (12th) 9-12h30
M° Ledru Rollin et   sam;
 Faidherbe-Chaligny dim 9-
                        13h

✓ Forum des Hal
  M-Th. all d
  7, rue Pierre

couldn't find —
is this for real

Livres
Brassan
rue Brancion
Sat, Sun - 9h—

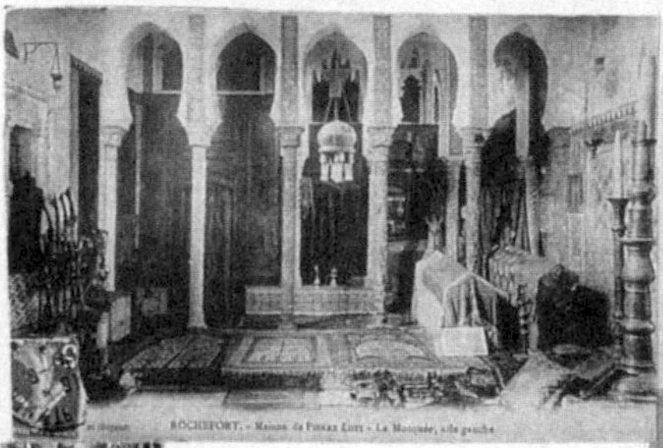

? Des Sablons à Neuilly sur Seine
  Brocantes 19-21 mai   couldn't find
  (Axel)   not listed

les Puces de St-
M° Porte de Clig anc
 75018
730 - 19h Sat,
Le marché Jules
 livres, etc.
or 10 to 6 ?

ROCHEFORT - Maison de Pierre Loti - La Mosquée, côté gauche

CARTES POSTALES

François Magnin - 25,   Saint-Paul
   mardi au vendredi

Les Image de Marc   (75003), M° Chemin Vert
   mardi - samedi   Bréguet Sabin
                                                            Bastille

"La Galcante - 52, ru   Dany (de la part de
   12 - 19 - mardi -   Claude)

La France ancienne   rue Montmartre, Richelieu-
                                                                   Drouot

Les Archives de la Pr   75003   M° Rambuteau
   lundi - samedi.

ROCHEFORT — Cheminée dans la Salle
ROCHEFORT — Maison de Pierre LOTI — Le Mihrab dans la Mosquée
ROCHEFORT — Maison de Pierre LOTI — Chambre Arabe
ROCHEFORT — Maison de Pierre Loti — Cheminée dans la grande salle

Toyo "Jouets Anciens" 11-12, 13-19
   rue Vaugirard

On the Pierre Loti Trail

ROCHEFORT

I NO LONGER REMEMBER WHEN I FIRST CROSSED PATHS with the French author Pierre Loti, but once I made his acquaintance, I knew I would never let him out of my sight. Loti was a man committed to his obsessions: traveling, writing, marrying temporarily, and re-creating the exotic, whether from the past or from foreign lands. Although he lived until 1923, he remained firmly locked in the nineteenth century.

Loti was born Louis-Marie-Julien Viaud at Rochefort-sur-Mer in 1850. Rochefort, formerly a thriving naval town (boasting, in the nineteenth century, the longest industrial building in Europe, dedicated to making ship rope), is now several miles from the coastline and somewhat somnolent.

It was inevitable, given his family's ties with the sea, that Loti would become a naval officer. Between his many journeys around the world—to China, Japan, Egypt, Turkey, India, the South Pacific (where he was given his pseudonym by the Queen of Tahiti)—he lived in the house where he was born. Part of his enduring mythology is bound to this house, which he filled with medieval, Islamic, and Oriental splendor. During a visit to Damascus, he procured a mosque complete with mihrab, a feature used to indicate the direction to Mecca. It and an accompanying minaret, both cumbersome to ship and to install, are examples of Loti's remarkable attention to detail.

From his tour of duty in Peking following the Boxer Rebellion, he brought back some 150 outfits, later used as costumes for his guests at one of his legendary fancy dress balls. From Constantinople, he smuggled out the tombstone of his long-deceased Turkish mistress, whom he immortalized as Aziyadé in his book of the same name.

He transformed his house room by room to include a Chinese pavilion, a Japanese pagoda, a

ABOVE: *Pierre Loti.*

FACING PAGE: *Loti, in his Arab salon. Engraving by H. Dochy, after a photograph by M. Dornac.* Soleil du dimanche, *April 3, 1892.*

Gothic room, a Renaissance hall, a Turkish salon, an Arab divan, and the Damascus mosque, all hidden behind a drab, provincial facade. He frequently dressed in Turkish clothing and smoked a nargileh. On special occasions he insisted that his visitors act their parts, as participants at medieval feasts or Oriental balls. His French wife, Jeanne-Blanche Franc de Ferrière of Bordeaux, joined in the masquerades, though she otherwise showed no taste for exoticism.

The house and its many landscapes were Loti's attempt to be elsewhere always. They sustained an illusion of romance among the familiar, where, to him, romance did not exist. Loti's world was too large to be contained in a house in a small town in France, so he expanded that house through bewitching artifice to encompass the globe.

Into the early twentieth century, Loti and his house were publicized through postcards and *cartes de visite*. Engravings of Loti reclining on a low sofa dressed in a burnous and turban were published in weekly papers, enhancing his reputation as a romantic figure.

But even more than the pictures of him and his splendid home, his books poignantly express a longing for a time lost, for a love lost. Filled with sensual descriptions of atmosphere, the novels are unmistakably autobiographical, especially his *Aziyadé*, *Le Mariage de Loti*, and *Le Roman d'un spahi*. A passionate nostalgia also nourishes the travel accounts, including *Au Maroc*, *L'Inde (sans les Anglais)*, and *Le Caire*, though at times they are edged with a cutting humor.

The contemporary reviewer and novelist Edmund Gosse wrote, "For those who have passed under the spell of Loti, he is irresistible. He wields the authority of the charmer, of the magician, and he leads us whither he chooses."[1] Most of Loti's books remain popular in French and are reissued periodically in English.

The Maison Pierre Loti at 141 rue Pierre Loti still exists, despite Loti's instructions that his acquisitions be sold off after his death. For the Lotified, a visit there, though restricted by a guided tour in French, reveals something of the depths of the most exotic mind of nineteenth-century France.

1 Edmund Gosse, "Pierre Loti," 202.

Rochefort's Bouquinerie Pierre Loti, also on rue Pierre Loti, has an impressive collection of books by and about Loti. Those who are really serious will consider joining La Société des amis de Pierre Loti (The Friends of Pierre Loti) or traveling to Istanbul to stay at Hotel Pierre Loti, a characterless modern establishment, at Piyerloti Caddesi 5 near the Aghia Sophia. This establishment also has a Pierre Loti Café. Just as unauthentic but more atmospheric, because of its beautiful view of the Golden Horn, is the Pierre Loti Café in Eyüp, a suburb of Istanbul.

The Japanese pagoda, no longer in existence, at Loti's Rochefort house, c. 1910.

NAPLES

1	2	3	4	5	6	7
2				10	12	14
3				15	18	21
4				20	24	28
5	10	15	20	25	30	35
6	12	18	24	30	36	42
7	14	21	28	35	42	49
8	16	24	32	40	48	56
9	18	27	36	45	54	63
10	20	30	40	50	60	70

MY EYES DRIFT UP FROM THE WALKWAYS to the walls, natural surfaces for posters—stapled, glued—poster on top of poster, layers from weeks, months, curling in on each other, trading colors, images, messages. My fingers act on their own: they reach out and tear at the weathered paper. Shredded loot fills my pockets. My notebooks bulge with these samples of detritus stamped by neglect and indifference. I'm in Naples, and my way of seeing has been turned ninety degrees.

Having trained as an archaeologist, I was taught to think that the past evolves as horizontal layers in the ground. Ash falls over bones, silt drifts over ash, plants grow in the silt and die and rot, shelters are built, then collapse, bones accumulate, bones are covered by ash. Wherever we live, we are inevitably atop some previous activity, whether geological, animal, or human. Digging down into the ground, we fall into history.

Naples taught me to look at vertical strata, for in Naples, human occupation is revealed on a large scale via posters. They transform the streets into the Museum of Daily Life. Layer upon layer of paper calls attention to saints' days, musical performances, plays, circuses, demonstrations, warnings, university talks, publications, items for sale, flats for rent. The benign climate and the protected aspects of the narrow streets give these posters a longevity they would be denied in London, Berlin, or Toronto. And Neapolitans are a lazy lot: it is much easier to plaster over old posters than to scrape them off and start

ABOVE: *A page torn from a* quaderno *(notebook), and found on a Naples street, along with a flea-market photograph.*
FACING PAGE: *Because of frequent elections, political posters are well represented in Naples.*
PREVIOUS SPREAD: *Scraps from a Naples wall transferred to my notebook.*

Two rescued objects, a map and a watch, both as dilapidated and as picturesque as Naples itself and, like Naples, back in use after years of neglect.

afresh. If there is a municipal initiative to clean the walls occasionally, it isn't apparent.

Naples is a layered city. Older structures expand, zigzag, and lean with additions, new facades, more doors, blocked-up windows. Why tear down a building and rebuild from scratch when it can be patched? A whole street is testimony to this attitude: Via Case Puntellate, Street of the Propped-Up Houses, in the Vomero district. But even more profound, in both senses of the word, is the fact that the above-ground city is built on Greek and Roman foundations. Evidence of these foundations extrudes through the surface in surprising places: at the feet of Vincenzo Bellini's statue in the center of Piazza Bellini, in the cloister at San Lorenzo Maggiore on Via dei Tribunali, and in the outer courtyard of Santa Chiara on Via Benedetto Croce, to name but three examples. At least one scholar believed that this ancient heritage was apparent in the people themselves. The learned Canon Andrea de Jorio used Neapolitans of his time to identify gestures shown on Greek vases and Roman frescoes. His magnum opus was called *La mimica degli antichi investigata nel gestire napoletano (The Mimicry of Ancient People Interpreted through the Gestures of Neapolitans).*[1]

The layering can also be attributed to Naples's more recent history, not as an Italian city but as a city belonging to many countries. During its post–Greco-Roman years, Naples has been in the possession of Sicilian Normans, Angevins, Aragonese, Austrians, Bourbons, Bonaparte, and Bourbons again; finally, in 1860, it became part of Italy. A brief tour of the city's core reveals fine examples of many types of European architecture, from Gothic to baroque, from Renaissance to neoclassical. Damage from earthquakes, cleansing from plague and revolution, and the ever-present threat of the eruption of the great, confounding, disturbing Vesuvius to the south add a delirium to the overpowering atmosphere of visible history.

But how easy it is to lose track of oneself in this raucous, bewildering city. I wonder if anyone cares that I have purloined shreds of paper from posters, the messages of which expired last month or even last year? Still, it doesn't seem quite the thing to do, at least not in broad daylight and not in front of crowds of people. I therefore confine my work to the hours after dusk or to out-of-the-way streets that seem abandoned by all except the hangers of posters and strays like me. What this stratagem lacks in probity is more than made up for by sightseeing opportunities. The search for wall detritus has taken me into corners of Naples that I would wager most Neapolitans don't know or purposely avoid, and it has given me the material to turn my journals into unique souvenirs of a city like no other.

1 Luigi Barzini, *The Italians,* 63–64.

Between the Pages

I FIRST WENT TO BUDAPEST IN MAY 1997 as part of my research for my novel *The Sensualist*. I needed to visit the Semmelweis Medical Museum and to swim in the baths at the stately Gellért Hotel.

The tourist information agent at the train station had a warm, welcoming smile. She graciously *gave* me bus tickets and found me a room at an agreeable hotel run by former acrobats. The efficient and underutilized buses ran along broad, manicured boulevards. The architecture in the center—an eclectic mix of neoclassical and Art Nouveau, sprouting turrets and domes, ennobled with entablatures supported by massive Atlas or caryatid figures—gave a fitting grandeur to this once strategically important city. My stay was blessed with flawless blue skies and a temperature moderated by a lovely breeze.

A second visit a year later was to an almost completely different place. This time rain poured ceaselessly. Low, heavy cloud kept the pollution at nose level. The helpful tourist office agent had been replaced by a holdover from the Communist era who refused to book a room, give directions for how to make a phone call or find a phone number, sell bus tickets, provide a map, or admit that she worked in a tourist information office.

I figured out the phone system and got a room at the same hotel as the previous year, but the heat had been turned off for the season, so there was no way to dry clothing or get warm. If this had been my first visit to Budapest, I would have noticed little about the streets or architecture, as I was perpetually hunkered under an umbrella or packed into a crowded, steamed-up bus.

ABOVE: *Identification document for Györgyné Kiss, 1942–48.*

FACING PAGE: *The doorbell system at a Budapest apartment.*

Unchanging through rain or shine, however, were the well-stocked and plentiful *antikvárium*, the antiquarian and secondhand bookstores. The first thing that struck me about them was the stack of plastic baskets—the sort you find at supermarkets—inside the entrance to each one. The second thing was that customers were carrying these baskets and filling them up. Either the citizens of Budapest are voracious readers or they love being surrounded by books.

Although most of the books in Budapest bookstores are in Hungarian, German, or Latin, none of which I understand, I was instantly beguiled. I too grabbed a basket and launched into a book-buying spree that ended with the purchase of a duffel bag to hold them

all. When my loot and I arrived home, I had to face up to the fact that I could not read a single book.

I had started out small, having discovered that most of the bookstores had drawers and bins filled with old documents, including personal identification cards, receipts, letters, telegrams, report cards, and coupons, adorned with photographs, signatures, seals—everything that the ephemera lover dreams of. My purchases graduated to smallish books—university theses on *materia medica*, psalters, ledgers, and unidentifiable works. Soon I was considering such weighty tomes as *Historia Ecclesiastica*, 1751, and a stunning, completely handwritten work entitled *Planum seu Opus Deputaonis Rece sub Presidio Ctis Christophori Niczky*, 1797, in which 234 pages were filled with descriptions of legal cases. Over the last two hundred

Identification booklet for Grauka Öry Erzsébet, 1917–18.

years, this latter item has been in a fire, doused in water, and stored away, but its pages still respond to the fingers with a crisp snap, and the texture of the paper is seductively coarse. The spine, pictured on the right, no longer disguises and protects the book; through the damage it shows the signatures, the binding twine, and the layers of leather and gilt.

I rationalized these purchases by calling them "inspiration" and by planning to incorporate them into my own work, and I bought them from the marked-down shelves, where stood the broken, the emblazed, the irretrievably obscure.

Because I was paying no more than four or five thousand forints for a book (twenty to thirty dollars at the time), and often much less, I ignored the subject matter—not being able to read it anyway—and made my selections solely on the basis of tactile and visual appeal. Imagine my delight, then, when later opening *Imperatores Ottomanici (Ottoman Rulers)*, volume one, 1760, to be reminded that it had a spectacular two-color title page. And I had completely missed the decorative engravings scattered throughout: mythological creatures, crosses between Greek gods and Christian angels, heralding the arrival of Crusader sailing ships; a Turk fending off a powerful eagle; the Sultan receiving pots of gold from his subjects; Turks firing cannons at the Crusaders' ships. I felt so lucky I could barely stand it. Then the real treasure, not something that had been created with the book, but something added later: a playing card stuck between the pages. Suddenly, this was no longer just a book off the shelf in a bookstore; someone had owned it, read it before.

The find set off an investigation into playing cards. I took the card to the playing-card expert in London's Camden Passage, referred to in an earlier chapter. He told me that it was part of a tarock—also known as tarocchi—pack from about 1850; whoever had left it in there had probably consulted the book some hundred years after it had

been published. A complete set consists of seventy-eight cards and would now cost about a thousand pounds, so adding the rest of the pack to my single card, shown on the facing page, even if I could find a similar set, was out of the question.

I have saved the items that I've salvaged over the years: pressed plants, menus, newspaper clippings, snapshots, business cards, sketches, prescriptions, and pages torn out of other books. They make me think of the things that I've inadvertently used as bookmarks: receipts, library patron record slips, greeting cards, notes. When I reread a book that has not been off my shelf in a decade or two and find, for instance, an old-style bus transfer, I am reminded of how fast things change and how impersonal many of them have become. There is nothing unique about today's receipts, and the printing on them fades in a very short time; notes are more often computer-generated laser pages than handwritten missives; and when was the last time anyone had the leisure to pick a flower and press it between the pages of a book?

ABOVE: *A sketch and a photograph found in the pages of a Hungarian book.*

FACING PAGE: *The tarock card and the book it was found in.*

Seminarium in Pesth

D E

UNO, &

RNATIONE,

&

TUTIBUS THEO

I.

natura nobis impressa est ; inde

DEI constitutivus.

ta divina ad essentiam comparata ,

natura rei , sed virtualis eaque i

hibus rebus intime præsens est, no

tia; en minicula... & solus æternus.

IV. Ab intellectu creato per naturæ vires videri
gloriæ videri potest, non tamen comprehendi.

V. Intellectus creatus adjutus lumine gloriæ ad vi
autem illud sive sit donum animæ intrinsecum , sive ub
lis concursus, creaturæ tamen nulli connaturale , ac deb

VI. Visio in beatis inæqualis est , cujus inæqualitas
rum tanquam causa morali , & inæqualitate luminis glori
vero a majori vel minori intellectus perspicacia.

VII. In DEO est veri nominis scientia , eaque per
prehendit , & omnia a se distincta tum existentia , tu

The Grand Bazaar

ON THE 21ST OF AUGUST, 1924, MONSIEUR Spadaros of Constantinople borrowed thirty Turkish lire from the widow Madame Marie Chelli. He signed a paper promising to pay back the sum by the 6th of September, but we'll never know whether he did.

It is a fluke that his notarized IOU was preserved in a stack of old papers in an antique store in Istanbul's Grand Bazaar. For such a long-lived and huge market—it consists of some four thousand shops, covering several square miles—it is surprisingly difficult to find documents and photographs. And when they do surface, the starting prices are astronomical.

The documents found in this store have no discernible historical importance, yet the information contained in them can trigger an Eric Ambleresque reverie. Why did Spadaros, probably a Greek, write his note in French? Were the Turkish notations added by the notary? Why did he need the money, and what would thirty lire have bought at the time? Was he a gambler? Was this loan his last chance to pull himself together?

What nationality was Mme Chelli? If she wasn't Turkish, what had brought her to Constantinople? Did she keep a rooming house, and was Spadaros one of her guests? She clearly did not trust his word that he would pay her back; she made him spend sixty-four kurus (less than one lira) to get the note drawn up.

The papers among which Spadaros's IOU was found were stained, torn, creased, and dusty, but I went through them one by one, initially looking for travel documents as part of my research into women's travel in the Middle East. I was soon caught up in the stories of the many nationalities represented in the stack. Two white Russians, Morris Ambaloff and

ABOVE: *A detail from a photograph of a Turkish family, c. 1910.*
FACING PAGE: *Old documents found in Istanbul's Grand Bazaar.*

Sté ANONYME TURQUE D'...
ET D'ENTRE...

Ga...

32.
Empire Ottoman
Carnet de passeport
Valable pour un an

Ann...

American Near East
Agence de

Receipt

    Received from Had...
of a parcel of 234...
Marks A H   Nº ...
carried from Ne...
American ...
twenty five, ...
    The ...
of 25 %...

Nicolai Ponomareff, were certified—in French, German, and
Turkish—to work in Ankara in 1924 by Herr Glaser, the Chief of
Construction in Constantinople. Hadji Dimitriadis, a Turk or
Albanian, paid $225 to the American Near East & Black Sea Shipping
Line in 1922 for a delivery of sugar from New York, a sum estimated
to be a quarter of the total value of the shipment.

There was a carbon copy of a letter from the commissioner of the
British High Commission to the head of the Allied Police. Acting as
a representative of the Allied High Commissions that also included
Italy and France, the commissioner suggested that the Allied Police
not enforce a Turkish court decision involving Abd-ul Rahman
Houloussi and Mayer & Cie. A translation of the letter in Turkish
was attached. Of what was Abd-ul Rahman accused? Or what had he
accused Mayer & Cie of doing?

More relevant to my research were several travel documents I
also happened upon. A passport issued to twenty-six-year-old Basile
Choros Sottiri in 1922 was drafted in French and Turkish and certi-
fied by the director of the Bureau of Passports for Albania in Turkey.
Better still was a passport issued on the 8th of April, 1922, to Mme
Feiga Berenbain and her four children. It allowed them to go from
Theodessia (now Feodosiya, in the southeastern Crimea in Ukraine)
to Constantinople. It was signed by representatives of Britain,
France, Italy, and Ottoman Turkey.

And finally, there was a document that I cannot decipher. It was
written on a standardized form with the Sultan's *tugra* (official
signature) at the top, a fiscal stamp on the right, and a darkened
photograph of a beautiful young woman on the left. It is signed by
at least two persons, including one Onnik Missiry. The imagination
takes flight with another Missiry, the once-famous former dragoman,
or interpreter, to the 1830s traveler Alexander Kinglake and later the
owner of one of Constantinople's most celebrated hotels, the
Angleterre. Was Onnik Missiry related to him?

These documents dated from before and during the time Turkey
was declared a republic, in 1924. The earliest of them were still under
the Sultan's seal; the alphabet had not yet been changed in Atatürk's
modernization of his country, and foreign governments were heavily

involved in its administration. Greeks, Armenians, French, Arabs, Italians, Germans, Russians, British, and, of course, Turks, gave the city its worldliness and complications.

Today Istanbul retains its intense cosmopolitan feel. The observer who spends an hour watching the faces of passersby along the walkway near the Galata Bridge will be rewarded with a sampling of complexions and features from around the globe. Clothing ranges from traditional vests and *shalwar* (Turkish trousers) to blue jeans or miniskirts, from the top of the fashion scale to the bottom and all parts between; extreme poverty and wealth reside side by side. Old-fashioned pudding shops sit next to trendy bistros where reservations must be made well in advance. Newsstands sell glossy magazines advertising high-priced Anatolian carpets, Iznik pottery, and Ottoman miniatures opposite twenty-first-century furnishings. Young girls in baggy pantaloons, plastic sandals, and frayed sweaters sit on the sidewalk along Divan Yolu near the Aghia

Sophia, offering simple caps that they knit while waiting for customers.

Nowhere in Istanbul does the world come together so vividly as in the Kapali Çarsi, the Grand Bazaar. This maze has existed in the same location since the fifteenth century, surviving attack, fire, and economic depression. As is usual in Middle Eastern markets, the bazaar is divided into sections, each devoted to its own specialty: leather, meerschaum, shoes, metalwork, spices. Within sections, the goods at any one shop are almost indistinguishable from those at the others. This is magpie heaven. Golden light reflects off glittery, silvery surfaces at every turn: shimmery coins sewn onto belly-dancing costumes; thick green, blue, or red glass-globed hanging lamps; brightly polished copper and brass trays, urns, vases, knives, bowls. That much of what is for sale here is new and made for tourists does not diminish the appeal.

However, the innermost market, the Iç Bedesten, is packed with unique and precious Ottoman objects: mother-of-pearl inlaid tables, diamond-studded daggers, nargilehs of crystal and porcelain, silks embroidered with fine gold thread. The contents of any shop in this cavern of Ali Baba would set up a would-be Pierre Loti in style.

For those who have not girded themselves to buy something, plunging into a shop takes nerves of steel—for entry leads to bargaining and then, as soon as money is discussed, to buying. As long as you remain a window shopper, your wallet is safe, in spite of the insistent merchants who stand outside and hurl prices and welcomes at you. Depending on your mood, you might ignore the attention, or you might find it entertaining. Few shoppers, however, can dismiss the verbal haranguing or the arm grabbing of the dealers in leather goods. Avoid these sections altogether for a lower-stress visit to the bazaar.

The antique store with the documents was located at the end of a difficult-to-find alley, full of twists and turns and apparent deadends, on the perimeter of the market. In contrast to the more centrally located shops, with their glitter and vibrant colors, the shops along this alley offered broken-down cash registers, bottle stoppers, and friable paper charts and maps. Hardly exotic collectibles, but still highly interesting. The alley suddenly emerged from the market's covered confines into the daylight, where it seemed to become an ordinary, workaday place where housewives go to buy boxes of Gleam laundry detergent. It was tempting to turn back.

But a shop at the corner looked different. Maybe it was the shop sign, perhaps an intriguing hint of faded textiles. A glance inside the open doorway invited a closer look. The textiles that had tantalized were cushions and carpets, cloaks and dresses. One display cabinet was filled with Koran pouches, another with gold brooches and rings. My documents perched at the end of a table overloaded with knick-knacks. Junk sat next to precious-looking objects. Lamps hung from every part of the ceiling. Hangings divided the space into small dens, like bazaars within a bazaar. This was the first of several visits I made, and with each visit it became more apparent that I would never know just how much was contained in this treasure trove.

There was no hustle—at first there was not even a shopkeeper. Shortly after our arrival, however, an old man sauntered in from the street and gestured widely to us to feast our eyes. This was the owner. It turned out that he was from a region of Turkey close to the

Syrian border, and he was more at home in Arabic than in Turkish. His sons, who arrived later, both spoke Turkish most comfortably, though their English was fluent and idiomatic. The elder son had taken to the antique trade with enthusiasm. He haunted the auction houses for anything that might be added to the shop but especially sought turn-of-the-century clothing from Anatolia and Istanbul. Over tea and negotiations for a jacket and *shalwar*, he showed me catalogs from past Istanbul auctions with production values worthy of Sotheby's or Christie's. He pointed to a photo of a lovely three-paneled dress from the early twentieth century, then leaped over to a rack of clothes where that same dress was hanging. "Look!" he exclaimed. "The auction tag is still on it!"

This young man is one of the new Grand Bazaar merchants. Unlike his father, who is content to wait for goods to come to him, he goes out and seeks them. He understands the international market and is comfortable with the Internet and with long-distance transactions. But otherwise he takes after his father. All merchants, representing untold generations from the same family, are canny men—for the trade in Turkey is still a man's occupation. They are confident that they, and then their descendants, will be in the same spot for centuries to come, and they are in no rush to sell anything of real value unless they can get the right price. Whether dealing in silver, gold, gems, inlaid furniture, pipes, textiles, or even old papers, they know their stuff and they know it well; it is in their blood.

Bazar de Stamboul,
Maison Sadullah & Cie.
Photograph by Guillaume
Berggren, c. 1890.
Courtesy Library of
Congress.

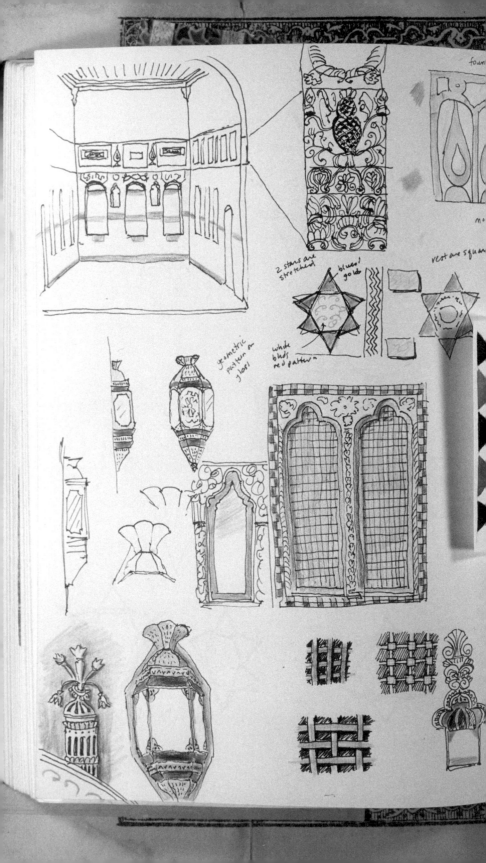

foun

2 stars are
stretched

blues/
gold

rest are square

geometric
pattern on
glass

white
birds
red pattern

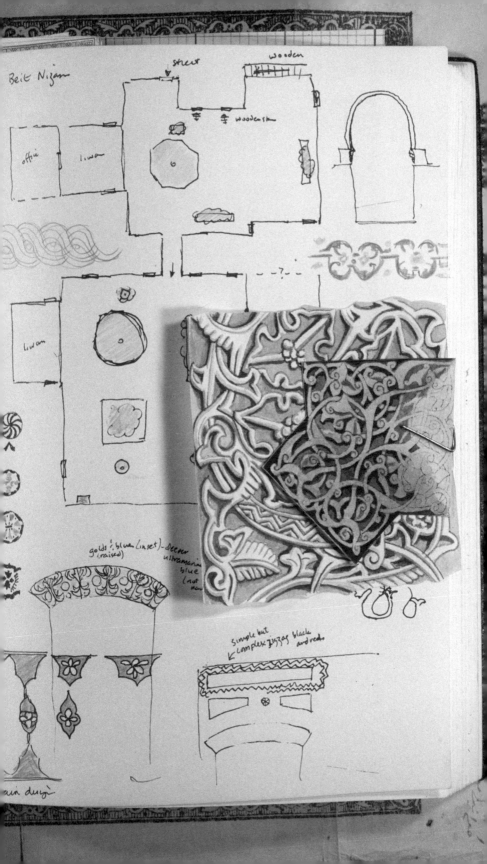

Beit Nizam

street

wooden

woodencish

offic

liwan

6

liwan

golds & blue (inset)-deeper ultramarine blue (not...)

simple but complex zigzag black and reds

main design

Rewarding Failure

FOR ANYONE PRONE TO DAYDREAMING about the past, the word "Damascus" is irresistible. It has been called the oldest continuously occupied city in the world, but its verdant gardens and elegantly ornamented buildings were even more renowned than its antiquity. At the peak of its beauty, it is said, Damascus was an oasis so heavenly that the prophet Mohammed turned away from it for fear of finding it better than God's heaven. For the early traveler, having crossed the inhospitable barren land that surrounds the city, to pass through one of the nine gates must have seemed like entering paradise itself.

Although today the city's magic is well hidden by concrete, traffic, and all the other ills that plague the modern world, the past asserts itself. In the old city, a bustling restaurant, filled at almost any hour with animated university students drinking tea, smoking apple-flavored *shishas* (the current word for nargilehs, or hubbly-bubblies), and checking their e-mail, was once a private home typical of those built over two hundred years ago. Its high ceilings, spacious salons, and wooden doors and shutters, all painted or carved with traditional intricately interlocking geometric designs, have been lovingly maintained. Jasmines and climbing roses twist along the first-floor balcony, dense and gnarly as though they had been planted when the house was first built. A young woman absently dips her hand into the cool water of the marble fountain that sits in the center of the courtyard. She's contemplating the table in front of her, laden with bowls of olives and dips, baskets stacked with flat breads, glasses of orange or pomegranate juice. Waiters—in traditional vests and sashes, woven in thin

ABOVE: *A sketch of an Iznik tile. These Turkish tiles were used to decorate the finer old buildings of Damascus.*

FACING PAGE: *A view toward the Umayyad Mosque, through the Roman gate.*

PREVIOUS SPREAD: *Sketches made in Damascus.*

2. Damaskus Ommajadan Moschee. RömischeBa

stripes of reds, yellows, and greens—dash about with trays of food and extra charcoal for the *shishas*.

The contrasts between the past and present are also evident as the sleek long-distance buses, equipped to show the latest Egyptian movies and Mr Bean episodes, pull into Baramkeh bus station, where tickets are still written out by hand, and waiting rooms are nothing more than space on a hard bench in one of the many booking offices.

Like so many others, I succumbed to the spell of Damascus and decided it was the best setting for my novel *The Lives of Shadows*. The plot involved an old house that had been lived in by generations of the same family.

My research had begun subconsciously in 1978, during my first trip to Syria. At that time, I fell in love with the architecture of the Middle East, especially as it was applied to the beautiful houses. The most attractive feature of these houses is that they hide their beauty from passersby. Their facades are crumbly, dingy, homely. Between the dangling electrical wires, peeling paint, and crumbling brick, most of them seem about to fall down. The doors are of roughly hewn planks knocked together with rusty nails and secured with corroded locks. But through these humble doors is another world, centered on peaceful courtyards, lushly planted with citrus trees, roses, and vines. A family of modest means may have only one courtyard; well-off families have up to three: one for women, one for receptions for men, and the last for the washing and cooking. Off the courtyards are salons with high ceilings for summer and low ceilings for winter. Raised sitting platforms strewn with cushions occupy a portion of these salons, often with fountains at the base. In some houses, rooms are decorated with painted scenes of cities, imaginary or real; in other houses, rooms are ornamented with geometric designs in golds, deep reds, greens, and blues. These rooms are built to give comfort to the body and to the eye.

Although many other Islamic cities are blessed with their share of such buildings, the houses of Damascus's old quarter are among the most accessible and the most elaborate in extent and decoration.

I prepared myself for my return to Damascus by studying every-thing I could about the city and its houses. My novel was set in the

76. Damaskus Eingang zum Suk Hamidie Bazar

1920s to 1940s, so I focused on the Damascus of those years. I bought old *Baedeker's* and *Cook's* guides and from them learned about the Cosmograph Cinema, La Rotonde Restaurant, Dimitri's Café, and the Victoria Hotel.

ABOVE: *A view of the old city of Damascus, c. 1914.*

NEXT SPREAD: *Houses in Damascus, 2002.*

I learned about the various *suqs*, the markets that make up a large portion of the old city, and compared early twentieth-century photographs of them with more current photographs. As in many Middle Eastern cities, they were, and still are, divided into specialties: the Attarin for perfumes, the Bazuriye for sweets, the Harir for silks, and the Hamir and Khail for donkeys and horses. Every section had its mosque or mosques, some so humble the muezzin announced the call to prayer at the street-level door; others, such as the Umayyad Mosque with its grand courtyard and three minarets, so significant that they became sites of pilgrimage. And each quarter had its *hammam*, its public bath, fed by the waters of the Barada River.

I knew how much it cost to take a taxi from the train station to the Victoria Hotel, what movies were playing, what records you could buy, where you could find the best pistachios, all the stuff of daily life. I began to feel as though I could make my way around the Damascus of 1920 more ably than I could make my way around my own city of today.[1]

1 For example, in 1912, a taxi cost six to eight paras. The para was a fraction of a Turkish medje. On October 23, 1922, a Monday, *L'Aiglonne* played at the Cosmograph on rue Damas, at the grand opening of the renovated *Salle d'hiver*. The singers Oum Kaltsoum and Mohamed Abdelwahab were as popular here in the 1920s as they were in Egypt.

I studied old surveys and located the houses—*beit,* as they are known in Arabic—that I might use as a model for the house in my book. My head was filled with their names: Beit Shamiyyeh, Beit Barudi, Beit Aq'aad. I read about the families who lived in them: Muslims, Christians, Jews; intellectuals, political agitators, religious leaders, merchants.

When I returned to Damascus, I set out to find the perfect quarter and the perfect house for my story. I noted the street names and checked them against the most comprehensive map I could find. Because virtually all of the posted street names differed from those printed on my map, I made many corrections.

Name changing was understandable, given the sometimes volatile succession of governments, but why had all of them changed? Even the main street, Midhat Pasha, which turns into the Street called Straight or Suq at-Tawil, had different names; on the map it was Al-Fusqar, changing halfway along to As-Suq al-Kabir. If the gate names—Bab al-Jabiya, Bab as-Saghir, Bab Sharqi—had not been the same as they are today, I would have thought I had a map for a different city. This map was dated 1924, but I guessed it was a reprint from the late 1800s. When I asked a librarian at the Institut Français about the discrepancies, I was told that it was a reprint of one that had been created in the 1200s. Because the layout of the streets and buildings was identical to those of today's old city, the sense of dislocation I experienced while following this map was profound.

By systematically going down each street, lane, and cul-de-sac, I had explored the city as thoroughly as could be done in a short visit. My meandering took me past Roman ruins and into coffee houses, bakeries, baths, mosques, churches, restaurants, private houses, old-folks' homes, shops, art galleries, schools, stables, and gardens. I learned about military service from young custodians of public buildings, drank tea with geriatrics, gossiped with Franciscan friars, and exchanged civilities with Muslim clerics.

The old city, confined by its ancient walls, is less than a mile long—but much happens here. The traffic is chaotic on the few thoroughfares. And even in the narrower streets, immense, impeccably polished Chevrolet coupes from the 1940s and '50s manage to jam

themselves in, along with Citroëns of the same vintage. In the tiny Christian quarter, Bab Tuma, where cocktail bars and the St Ananias Chapel are popular attractions, elaborate grottoes dedicated to the Virgin are tucked away in back streets. In the neighboring Jewish quarter, Harat al-Yahud, fewer than one hundred Jews remain out of a former population of around four thousand after the Syrian government granted exit visas in 1993. Now their houses, once the pride of Damascus, written about by many visitors to the city, are either occupied by Christians or Muslims or are becoming dilapidated and uninhabitable.

A detail of a map of the Damascus medina, with street names dating to around 1200, but still surprisingly useful. Revised by K. Wulzinger and C. Watzinger, Damaskus, Die Islamische Stadt (Berlin: Vereinigung Wissenschaftlicher Verleger, 1924).

I was lucky to have a personal escort on numerous sorties. Fatie Darwish, an Englishwoman who has lived in Damascus since the late 1940s, took me in hand, as she has with so many visitors, and shared her rich and colorful knowledge of the city.

The research I had already done and the explorations of the streets were all important, but I thought it necessary to go to the city archives, where, I presumed, old deeds would be stored. My efforts broke down at this point. The only archives I heard of, the only ones that anyone could direct me to, were always closed. The librarians at the Institut Français, the Assad library, and the British Consul, all helpful in other ways, could suggest no other sources.

I turned to the antique stores on the Suq al-Qabaqbiyeh, along the south side of the Umayyad Mosque. Most of the shops there are holes-in-the-wall, so tiny that everything they contain seems to be on display. They burst with glassware, jewelry, curios, everything but paper. When I asked about documents, however, merchants pulled shoeboxes out from under desks and envelopes from behind shelved books. They unfolded vellums upon which were written the poems of the Persian Hafiz. They unrolled Turkish documents called *firmans*, decrees issued in the name of the Sultan: permission to travel, permission to establish a *wakf* (charity). They opened up exercise books filled with Antar's escapades, written in schoolchild Arabic, and shuffled scraps of calligraphy practice, all tempting in their own right but not related to the buying or selling of houses.

Yet even in failure, there was luck. I had been looking for information about singers from the 1920s and '30s and, in one shop, discovered a photograph of an Aleppan singer, Ajfan al-Amir. In the same place, I found *cartes d'identité*, identification documents, issued during the 1930s, which I hadn't even thought of needing, but which now seemed indispensable.

Moving along to the Sharia Qaimariyeh, east of the mosque, I found several curio shops tucked in between the carpet shops that this street is known for. Their windows were obscured by shelves warped with heavy glass bottles and painted ceramic jugs. One could only appreciate the quantity of goods in these stores by methodically inventorying their contents: record albums, framed photographs, pots, furniture—all dusty, broken, dear, and desirable.

In the corner of one shop window, the dealer had stacked several glass lantern slides. When held up to the imperfect light, the Pyramids became visible in one, the temple of Baalbek in another. Emerging through the cracks and disintegrating emulsion of these images were travelers and their guides from the 1920s.

These unexpected treasures helped me build the past, but I still wanted a deed.

A Serendipitous Find

ALEPPO

I HAD SPENT TOO MANY DAYS IN DAMASCUS looking for phantom house deeds. If I was to see anything else of Syria, it was time to leave. I made my way first to the desert ruins of Palmyra, then to the Euphrates town of Deir az-Zor. From there I went to Aleppo in northern Syria.

Aleppo is a frantic city made up of a hodge-podge of building styles, the most attractive of which—the two- and three-story wooden Turkish houses with cantilevered and latticed balconies—are slowly disappearing. The streets are always busy with cars, trucks, buses, pedestrians. Goods spill out of stores and warehouses onto the sidewalks, such as they are. There are few refuges from the noise and pollution.

Aleppo's center can be roughly divided into three main sections: the modern city, the Christian quarter, and the old city, or medina.

In the modern city, east of the main artery, Baron Street, and around the Bab al-Faraj clock tower, Russian textile traders make their temporary homes in dilapidated hotels, where the lobbies burst with bundles of Aleppan cottons. Around the corner, juice vendors line one street, cheap restaurants another. Hustlers beckon at the doors of dubious clubs. Shopping arcades lead off the traffic-clogged streets, providing temporary relief from the noise and the glare. The stores in these arcades display mannequins behind plate-glass windows, and some stores even have neon signs. Although their style is reminiscent of North America in the sixties, their organization is decidedly Middle Eastern. One arcade consists of shoe and handbag stores, each identical to its neighbor, each selling exactly what its neighbor sells.

Papers and photographs found at the Orient House, an antique shop in the Jdideh quarter of Aleppo. The top photograph shows the entrance to Aleppo's famous Citadel. On the bottom left is a view of the clock tower at Bab al-Faraj.

Farther on is the Christian quarter, also called Jdideh, meaning "new." It was established in the fifteenth century for Armenian and Maronite traders and their families. Calm and residential, it has narrow cobblestone streets that discourage traffic and encourage strolling. The reward for a morning's exploration is lunch or a coffee in one of the old stone houses recently converted into stylish restaurants and hotels.

The old city, however, is Aleppo's big draw. The *suqs* here, at the base of the imposing early-thirteenth-century citadel, are even more extensive, busy, and cosmopolitan than those of Damascus. Significant portions of the streets are covered with vaulted stone roofs. Domes at junctions and in certain courtyards are laced with small glass-covered holes to let in light. If all of the streets were laid end to end, they would stretch for more than four miles, and even though they are roughly on a grid, they are still labyrinthine. Merchants come here from all parts of the Middle East, and one hears Turkish, Kurdish, and Persian alongside Arabic. For those wishing to buy a Bedouin tent or several tons of Aleppan olive-oil soap, this is the place.

The hustle can be intense. Touts are fluent in Russian, German, French, and English, and some, no doubt, have a facility with Dutch, Chinese, or Swahili. And there are several young men who can speak knowledgeably about almost any city in the world. "Where are you from?" one of these omnipresent wizards asks. "North Vancouver," you answer smugly, thinking no one knows anything about North Vancouver. "Ah," he replies, "Is it still nice along Lonsdale Avenue?" You are positive he has never left Syria in his life, yet you quickly learn during your frequent encounters with him that no matter what town or city you name, whether Cape Town, Norfolk, or Guangzhou, he will talk about it as if he has lived there for several years.

While exploring this vast network of lanes and courtyards, I wandered into the Khan al-Gumruk (or Jumruk), a large open courtyard—it is Aleppo's largest khan, or caravanserai—where customs agents once worked. It was built in the late sixteenth century and for a time housed the consuls of France, England, and Holland. Silks and

cottons are now the dominant merchandise sold here. This khan, like others in the old city, is ringed by two-story buildings and is cut off from the main market by a narrow passageway and an immense wooden gate that was formerly closed at night or during times of unrest.

A wall in Aleppo with layers of peeling paint and paper.

I chanced to pick up a piece of pale yellow paper lying on the ground. It had been torn from a printed form and was covered in writing, not only Arabic but French as well, a language that was used in official documents during France's twenty-some years in Syria. There were more fragments scattered about, each apparently part of the same sheet. I could read words such as *domicile* and *immeuble*, French for "residence" and "building." The scraps were too small to make any sense individually, so I bought a roll of sticky tape and went back to the hotel, where I could spread the papers out and try to piece them together. Assembled, they became a portion of a document from the French Mandate of the 1920s to '40s, the time period

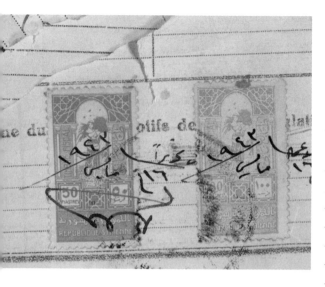

of my book. I still wasn't sure what they represented, but I had my hopes. I needed to find more.

As I walked to the khan the next day, I told myself that the place would have been swept clean, that the garbage would have been picked up. How lucky I was, then, to spot a small wastebasket tucked away in a corner, stuffed with more pale yellow papers. I began poking through them. Then, realizing how odd I must look, I asked around to find out who owned the wastebasket. This question brought a small crowd of workers and customers. Why, they asked, would I want old torn-up paper? One man pointed to a stain—spilt coffee—and shook his head in disgust.

My explanation made no sense to them. The French Mandate was long ago; I should buy new paper. Then I noticed a tax stamp affixed to one of the fragments and showed them that. They immediately understood an interest in stamps and helped me look for more. One fellow laughingly suggested I pay them ten Syrian pounds for the stamp; I agreed—if they would pay me ten Syrian pounds for tidying up their khan. We dumped the works into a plastic bag, and I left with my haul, a nearly complete eight-page deed dating from 1937 to 1943.

ABOVE AND FACING:
Pieces of the house deed
found at the Khan al-
Gumruk, Aleppo.

Références Cadastrales

Section ___ Feuille N°

Lieu-dit on O

ÉTAT DE SYRIE

DIRECTION GÉNÉRALE
DES SERVICES FONCIERS
ET DES DOMAINES

Conservation Foncière

(سند التمليك)

TITRE DE PROPR

5- حمى العقار (قيود سجل

بجموع القيمة | Con

Valeur totale

باب الترقين والتمر

Motifs des radiati
et mentions

ière

N° b ⟶ ف

s du Titre

تاريخ ومحل الولادة

e et lieu de naissance

الاوراق

صحيفة (السطر الاول)

ion par fusionnement

ment

فراز

قة (السطر الاول) والتعد

cation par fusionneme

ar fu

Section

Radi

Mo

en-Fonds
dastrale de

Three Dollars a Day

IN THE MID-1970S, THE EGYPTIAN GOVERNMENT required foreign visitors arriving at the Cairo airport to change US$150 into Egyptian pounds. I had been traveling on five dollars a day up to that point, and I was planning to stay in Egypt for a month, so this amount struck me as reasonable. My only concern was that the rate would be unfavorable, which it turned out not to be, except when compared with the black market.

For about ten cents, my travel companion and I took the airport bus to Maydan at-Tahrir, the busy square in the center of the city, then walked some distance to the youth hostel on Sharia Abdel Aziz as-Saud. The hostel charged us the equivalent of forty cents a night. The next day, we found that a filling meal of pitas with vegetables and meat, along with rice pudding and tea, cost less than twenty cents. A ferryboat ride to the city center set us back a piastre, a penny and a half. It was clear that for someone accustomed to traveling cheaply, $150 for a month was far too much money.

I began selling small amounts to other tourists, ten dollars here, fifteen dollars there. I splurged on movies, on beers at European-style hotels like Shepheard's and the Mena House, on sweets at Groppi's patisserie, on a full-course meal at the Café Riche, the favorite Cairo restaurant of President Gamal Abdel Nasser. At this time, Nasser had been dead for only six years, and the memory of his presence at the restaurant was still strong.

When we arrived in Luxor—after a ten-hour train ride that cost $3.75—I increased my efforts to unload my Egyptian pounds. I had time to consider what to spend them on, as we planned to stay in Luxor for a week. The usual souvenirs—brass trays and glass hubbly-bubblies—were either heavy or fragile, and I still had months left in my travels (in my

A street in Luxor's mercantile center, c. 1920.

A S W A N

mind, splurging did not include wasting money on shipping). Practical stuff—soap and toilet paper, for example—was pathetically cheap, especially since I helped myself to supplies from the washrooms at fancy hotels, a terrible habit that, thankfully, I have finally broken.

I did need new clothes, however. When I discovered an attractive street lined with tailor shops in the Luxor market, I decided to order a custom-made skirt. This was a big plunge, so I spent the better part of an afternoon selecting the shop. After looking at cloth and asking prices, I settled on a shop that looked no different from its neighbors. Nor did it carry anything that the others did not carry. I must have liked something in the tailor's manner.

The finished garments on display were mainly *abas*, long outdoor cloaks worn over indoor clothes. Because a skirt was not in the tailor's repertoire, I sketched out a picture to show the general style—including a waistband, a zipper, and two side pockets—and the length I wanted.

I chose the material by holding up bolts of cotton, trying to judge the effect in a small, tarnished mirror that hung over the washbasin. Once the cloth was decided upon and the price agreed to, the tailor commenced to work out the size. He hesitated when he put his tape measure around my middle. Instead of pulling it snug, he let it hang loosely. I did not think to measure my own waist for him, but I did wonder about his reluctance; after all, a tailor has to touch the customer, even a woman, at some point in the creation of a garment. I reassured myself that he would compensate for his delicacy with his expert eye. He told me the skirt would be finished the next day around the same time.

The skirt was ready as promised, but it was several sizes too large. When the error was discovered, the tailor ripped out the seams and resewed them to some even more haphazard estimate. To make matters worse, once the green-and-white striped, one-hundred-percent Egyptian cotton flannel that I'd chosen was sewn up, it had a marked resemblance to pajamas.

When I later wore the skirt to the house of an Egyptian friend, his father, a lawyer who had never met a North American budget traveler before, asked if it was really necessary to dress so badly.

That the awful skirt was topped by a hand-me-down, too-large army surplus shirt could not have ameliorated the effect, but it did help prevent the still oversize skirt from falling off. My footwear, too, had little appeal. I had clomped around in the same pair of Seven Star work boots nearly every day for six months, and they hadn't been anything to look at when I first put them on. I can't bear to think of what my socks were like.

By Aswan I had sold over fifty dollars and had squandered another twenty-five on two weeks of living expenses, leaving me with seventy-five dollars to spend. So I bought a thirty-dollar ticket for a hydrofoil ride up the Nile to the monuments of Abu Simbel. My traveling companion, who was about to head south to Khartoum and Kenya, laughed at my extravagance. Her third-class ticket to the town of Wadi Halfa, farther south, cost her five dollars, but her voyage, she later recounted, took a grim forty-eight hours.

The traveler attempts an ironic moment with her Luxor outfit, many months later in Fez, Morocco.

My journey took only five hours, but the passenger area of the hydrofoil was stuffy and hot. The other passengers were French and German tourists on guided tours, insular and self-absorbed as people on tours tend to become.

Abu Simbel, with the four colossal sandstone statues of Ramses II guarding the entrance to the main temple, was grander than anything I had seen up to this point, surpassing even the pyramids. The fact that it had been relocated after the flooding of the Nile added to the experience. Visitors could go into a passage that had been created between the inside of the monument and the exterior and see where all of the complex cuts had been made and the parts rejoined. I was supposed to accompany the tour, but as the guide did not speak English, I was allowed to wander on my own. The hydrofoil, unfortunately, was on a tight schedule, giving us less than two hours at the site.[1]

---

1 Reading later of how travelers such as Amelia Edwards camped out at Abu Simbel, coming and going according to their own schedules, almost made me weep at the frustrations of travel in the late twentieth century.

Back in Aswan, I gravitated to the weekly market. This was not a tourist attraction in any sense of the word. Goods for sale included faucets ripped out of demolished houses, plugged-up carburetors, heavily padded size 38E brassieres, rough towels in unhygienic shades of brown and yellow, Indian incense, and braying donkeys.

Still smarting from the dismissive once-over I had been justly given by my friend's father, I decided to buy some sandals to wear on special occasions. I chose the rubber flip-flops pictured on the left. Made in China, they could not have cost more than the equivalent of fifty cents. As an improvement on my appearance, they were a complete failure, yet they have proved their value many times over. They are almost thirty years old at the time of this writing, and I have worn them every summer and sporadically through the rest of the year—and they show no signs of giving up.

These indestructible sandals still evoke the market in the fresh early morning of a day that would reach a temperature of 100°F. The vendors had spread out over a bare, dusty field, their wares displayed on plastic and canvas tarps, in hemp bags, in stained and bursting boxes. The stink of donkeys and camels mingled with the sweet fragrance of freshly cut mint and the scent of shirts laundered in coarse soap.

Now, whenever I stumble upon such a market, no matter where, I check to make sure that flip-flops of this kind are still available. I just might need a new pair someday.

As for the skirt, I continued to wear it during my trip, chiefly over my blue jeans as an extra layer of warmth in the winter months. I brought it home with me, where it languished in a succession of closets until I forgot whatever attachment I may have once had for it and finally threw it out.

An Egyptian market,

c. 1910.

The Water Sellers

MARRAKECH

MY FIRST TRIP TO MOROCCO, IN THE WINTER OF 1976–77, was part of an aimless ramble, the main goal of which was to extend my time abroad by spending five dollars a day, or less. That goal was difficult to achieve even then, and it meant that I spent much energy economizing.

For an impoverished traveler, Morocco was a relief after Europe. It was not only cheaper but also warmer and more relaxed. The interlude there gave me a chance to eat better than I had for months and, more important, to assess my travels to date. I concluded that travel without purpose is fine for a while, especially if it gives the traveler the chance to see a variety of countries, but it wears thin. I decided that on future extended travels, I should set myself tasks. Whether it would be to learn a language, to study painting, or to volunteer as a gardener at the Alhambra, it did not matter. The point was to have a goal.

One of my few worthwhile pursuits during this trip was photography. I shot dozens of rolls of Kodachrome 64, the choice of many travel photographers because the price at that time included processing and a convenient mailing envelope. My photos were unremarkable, but the vibrancy of North African cities served as a valuable visual training ground.

Once I overcame my reluctance to ask people if I could take their photographs, I began amassing a small collection of portraits, one of which was of a pair of Marrakech water sellers. I had taken their picture in just the same way as hundreds of other tourists had. I snapped the shutter, capturing them proudly displaying their colorful water seller's gear, and paid them five dirhams each. We smiled at each other a lot, then said goodbye. I didn't know their names, how old they were, whether they had families.

ABOVE: *An herb seller's wall display, Marrakech.*

FACING PAGE:

Marrakech water sellers, 1976. Mohammed, "the gnaoui," is on the left.

They had been part of scenic Marrakech and no more, and I had been a tourist and no more.

Fourteen years later, I made my second trip to Morocco, taking a 1956 Rolleiflex twin-lens reflex camera, with the idea of creating a portfolio. The large ground-glass viewfinder and the 2¼-inch negatives gave me a greater sense of participating in the act of photography than using a 35-mm camera had. This was my first of many trips with the Rolleiflex. It was a heavy 5½ pounds, and I was paranoid about damaging or losing it. The twenty-odd rolls of 120 film I brought took up a disproportionate amount of space in my backpack, considering there were only twelve shots on a roll, and loading the film was slow and awkward. But it was worthwhile, not only for the resulting pictures, but for the interest it provoked from passersby, especially when they looked through the viewfinder.

I also wanted to create some continuity with the Morocco of my previous visit and to obtain a deeper impression of the country. I decided to find the two water sellers I had photographed in Marrakech and give them copies of the print.

The two men had been so old when I took their picture; would they still be alive? Did they make a respectable living selling water and posing for pictures? Did water sellers still exist in Morocco, or had they become obsolete? Finding them and giving them copies of the print was clearly the only way I would get answers to my questions.

I arrived in Marrakech in the spring of 1991. For three days— prints in hand—I searched without success through the *suqs,* the immense and tangled network of markets that spread out from the main square, the Djema el-Fna. The few water sellers about resembled neither of the two men in my photograph. Finally, I showed the print to one of these water sellers. He called to another to come over and help him explain that he recognized the men.

The second man introduced himself as Abd el-Salaam. He also recognized the water sellers and told me that they were both dead. The family of one of the men lived *An alley in the* some distance from town, but the family of "the *Marrakech medina.*

gnaoui," the black, lived in Marrakech, and he could take me to meet them.

I followed Abd el-Salaam through the medina, the old walled city. We went through the *suqs* to a residential area, following progressively smaller lanes. We were attracting attention, and I wish I could have watched us—the foreign woman with a red face, a self-conscious grin, and a large camera around her neck, walking a couple of paces behind the slow-gaited water seller, a tiny, wizened man burdened by his finery: wide-brimmed straw hat, multicolored tunic, heavy coin-studded pouch, and brass ladle and cups.

We turned into a dead-end alley narrower than the span of an arm, where a couple of giggling girls directed us to another alley. I waited at the entrance so that Abd el-Salaam could warn the deceased water seller's wife and sons that they were about to receive a visitor. A crowd of kids that had apparently been following us gathered around. Then noise burst out from the end of the cul-de-sac. Abd el-Salaam, surrounded by women, children, and young men, waved to me to approach. As I did, I held out the photograph, which was quickly snatched away and studied. It was passed from hand to hand, disappearing at times, then reappearing with much exclamation and finger pointing. I was hustled into the house and led through a small courtyard into the modest sitting room, where I was offered a seat on a divan. A small table appeared, then a tray. Glasses of tea and plates of biscuits were brought and handed out. In the excitement, the glasses were soon mixed up. Aziz, one of the water seller's sons, found a dog-eared copy of a magazine article in which a photograph of his father appeared. Here I learned that his name had been Mohammed, though everyone referred to him as "the *gnaoui.*" The article was clearly one of the few items they had to remember him by.

Abd el-Salaam sank back on the bench and took off his hat, wiping the sweat from his forehead, then freed himself of his pouch. These he handed to me so that I could study them and appreciate their weight. The straw hat was lined with felt and must have weighed ten pounds. The bag, with its thick leather, its massive straps, and all of its coins, could not have weighed less than twenty pounds. Abd el-Salaam quoted me a price for each item and pointed out the mid-twentieth-century dates on the coins and the brilliant colors of the band that circled the crown of the hat. He affably accepted my refusal to buy his gear, but I was saddened that he could make a better living by selling it than by wearing it.

Abd el-Salaam interpreted for me, as the family members spoke only Arabic. They told me the water seller had died six years earlier, at the age of fifty-three. I thought he had been much older. I asked Abd el-Salaam his age; he was fifty-five but looked an aged seventy.

The family was incredibly poor. Clearly the income of a water seller had not been enough to give them a comfortable life, even by Moroccan standards, and his death had no doubt made their situation all the more difficult. Giving them the photograph could not materially improve their lives, but I knew it would be treasured.

A Portable Arabic Typewriter

FEZ EL-DJEDID

ـــا السيـد اكـريسطـ
يــا أوشيـــــر بالبالغـ
‑4ـو5 مـايـو بـمـد يتــ
ـرار هـو تـصـريـح مـع
ـال الشـك فيهــا . ولقـ

WHEN I REVISITED MOROCCO IN 1994, I HAD been working on *The Tattooed Map,* an illustrated novel of a journey through that country. The manuscript was nearly finished and was to go to editing shortly after my return; on this last trip I would take more photographs and confirm some details.

Among the places I went back to was Fez, one of the most remarkable cities in North Africa. Fez is composed of three districts: the ancient Fez el-Bali, literally "Old Fez," established in the early ninth century; Fez el-Djedid, or "New Fez," dating from 1276; and the Ville Nouvelle, the late-nineteenth-century French quarter.

Fez el-Bali, walled like a fortress, absorbs the visitor into its labyrinthine alleys, packed with shops selling metalware, herbs, weavings, perfumes, and ceramics. The accessible *medersas* (Koranic schools)[1]—the courtyards of which are decorated with elaborately carved wood and stucco and intricately patterned *zellige* tiles—offer peaceful refuges from the havoc of the industrious leather dyers, porters, and touts. A living monument, Fez el-Bali is a UNESCO Heritage Site and is both home to some 200,000 Fassis and a destination for an ever-growing number of tourists.

Parts of Fez el-Djedid are built along spacious lines, with palaces, gardens, and tea shops and, unlike Fez el-Bali, have streets wide enough for cars. But this district also has its confusing, narrow alleyways, especially in the area known as the Mellah, meaning "salt," a word used throughout Morocco to designate Jewish districts. The Mellah in Fez is now mainly inhabited by poor Muslim families.

After a day spent in either "Old" or "New" Fez, the Ville Nouvelle, with its Art Deco hotels, train and bus stations, and French restaurants and cafés, offers a gentle return to modern-day reality.

---

1 In Morocco, mosques are open only to Muslims, so *medersas* are the one opportunity for non-Muslims to see inside a religious building.

While I was in Fez, it occurred to me that an Arabic typewriter might help me learn Arabic, a Sisyphean task I had set for myself more than a decade earlier. I began asking around for a portable, starting with stationers in the Ville Nouvelle. They recommended the market at the place des Alouites in Fez el-Djedid, where all kinds of old office equipment and furniture were for sale.

At the place des Alouites, French typewriters could be had for a song, but Arabic ones were nonexistent. Around the third shop or so, a man in his early thirties, seeing an opportunity to make a commission, approached and asked if I would let him find me a typewriter. His name was Mustapha, and he lived in the Mellah. I decided to accept his proposal.

He quickly determined that the remaining dealers at the market had nothing of interest, then told me of a scribe he knew who had several typewriters. We walked through Fez el-Djedid to an office opening onto Lalla Ghriba, a street wide enough to accommodate a median strip of unlicensed and anxious itinerant merchants. One of the distractions during my several hours in this office was to watch the merchants regularly sweep up their goods and disappear the instant word came that police were on their way.

The office was about six feet wide by eight feet deep, furnished with a desk, a bench, three chairs, a bare light bulb suspended from the ceiling, and some shelves holding a stack of paper and four typewriters. Sitting behind the desk was a tall, thin, neatly attired man, the scribe M'hammedi Alaoui M'hammed.

Mr M'hammed thought he might be persuaded to sell one of his typewriters, though only one of them was Arabic (the rest were French). He showed me the way that the Arabic one typed right to left, the arrangement of the keys, and the means by which one selected a terminal or medial version of any particular letter. He let me type a bunch of nonsense; then we had tea.

His typewriter was not portable; nor was it for sale after all. This fact put Mustapha at a disadvantage, as he could not make a commission if no money changed hands. He took off, promising to search around some more and to meet me the following day at Mr M'hammed's office.

I lingered while customers had their letters composed and typed. It occurred to me that I could use a letter typed in Arabic in *The Tattooed Map*. That night I wrote a police report in my best bad French, detailing the testimony of one of my characters about the disappearance of his female companion. I took this document to the scribe the next day and suffered his corrections to my French before he translated it into Arabic.

Two men came into the office and engaged Mr M'hammed in a loud, almost violent discussion. Then Mustapha arrived and waited quietly by my side until the yelling stopped. The men then took off but returned ten minutes later carrying a large, beat-up case, which they opened to reveal a splendid Olivetti portable typewriter. Mr M'hammed made room for it on his desk and slipped a piece of paper into it. He began typing, nodding as the letters flew onto the paper.

How much did they want for it? I was not prepared for the high price—three thousand dirhams, then the equivalent of $280—but he was not at all surprised, perhaps thinking of the two to four commissions that were no doubt included.

I also considered the commissions and realized that bargaining opportunities were limited. I picked up the machine and professed that I could not carry it; I typed out my name, then pointed out a deficiency in the carriage return mechanism. I knowledgeably mentioned that such typewriters were available in Casablanca for a thousand dirhams. These objections and others were countered with more shouting, finger pointing, and scowling. I was told that if I bought one for a thousand in Casa, I was to bring it back, as I could make another thousand by selling it in Fez. The price came down to 2,500, then 2,200; then they left. Soon they came back and haggled some more. I eventually—and, I hope, gracefully—wriggled out of buying the typewriter, but only when Mr M'hammed said he would consider buying it.

I paid Mr M'hammed for the translation, shook hands with the two men who had brought the typewriter, and took Mustapha out for a tea and gave him a token fee for his help. Later that day, while walking down the Talaa el-Kebira in Fez el-Bali, I heard someone calling my name. It was one of the men who had brought the typewriter to the scribe's office. He waved me into his own small office. There was the typewriter, sitting on his desk. He smiled and told me that the price was now 1,800 dirhams. By this time, I realized that the typewriter was an event for me, not an item that I should purchase, so I declined on the basis that it wasn't any lighter for being cheaper. We agreed that it was better for Mr M'hammed to buy it, as it would help his work, so all was well. I left with the sensation that no amount of sightseeing in Fez could ever have replaced the pleasure of looking for a portable Arabic typewriter.

The Forbes Museum

TANGIER

WHILE STAYING IN A SMALL BED-AND-BREAKFAST near London's Russell Square, I learned that the proprietress had grown up in Tangier and immigrated to England when she was in her early twenties. She needed no coaxing to describe the fantastic life she and her family had led. She reminisced about the literary scene, led by Paul and Jane Bowles; the wealth, seen in the palaces of Barbara Hutton and Malcolm Forbes; the cosmopolitan atmosphere, in the nightclubs, restaurants, and sensational parties; and the intrigue, for Tangier was a city on the edge, well outside of the rules of Europe and North America. It had been designated an international zone with a free port since 1923, and those who wanted to disappear could do so there without actually vanishing off the face of the earth.

I asked the hotel keeper if she ever went back. Her smile faded. Yes, she had been back, but no one but Moroccans lived in Tangier now. The city had lost its glitter; there was no longer any reason to return.

I can think of many reasons to go to Tangier—the markets, the history, the intensity—but tracking down the city's bygone international years has played a big part in my visits. I started with Walter Harris, the *Times* correspondent and unofficial English diplomat who not only covered the 1904 abduction of two American citizens, Mr Perdicaris and his stepson, Mr Varley, by Moulay Ahmed er-Raisuli, a handsome, educated Moroccan tribal chief and cattle rustler, but had himself been kidnapped by the dashing brigand, a man he called "a typical and ideal bandit."[1] My interest in this episode had been ignited by the movie *The Wind and the Lion*, and it

ABOVE: *A packet of postcards from Tangier, c. 1930.*

FACING PAGE: *A statue in the grounds of the Forbes Museum, 1991.*

1 Walter Harris, *Morocco That Was*, 181.

was of no consequence to me that the movie had been panned or that Candice Bergen had stepped into Mr Perdicaris's shoes. The important character was the Raisuli, and, in my eyes, Sean Connery played him extraordinarily romantically.

Walter Harris understated this account and all else that happened— raids, intrigues in the Sultan's court, international contretemps— during his years in Morocco, making the place seem all the more thrilling, and I believe that his columns helped establish Tangier as a refuge for the misfits of the twentieth century. His inventory of the Sultan's photographic equipment, hansom cabs, wigs, and ladies' undergarments from Paris would have attracted every itinerant salesman from Europe, but a host of other characters had already found a welcome. On one occasion Harris observed that

> the Sultan was playing bicycle-polo with some of his European suite, which included at this period an architect, a conjurer, a watch-maker, an American portrait-painter, two photographers, a German lion-tamer, a French soda-water manufacturer, a chauffeur, a fire-work expert, and a Scottish piper.[2]

Along with those attracted by the low cost of living, the company of other undesirables, and the absence of law and order came the high-flyers. A late arrival on the Tangier scene, Malcolm Forbes, the magazine magnate, was one of the richest of them all. Forbes came to Tangier in 1970, ostensibly to publish an Arabic-language edition of *Fortune*. His villa, the Palais du Mendoub in the swank Marshan district, overlooks the Atlantic and is distant from the claustrophobic medina. It is an enormous, whitewashed Moorish fantasy, sur-rounded by palm trees, tiled walkways, and hideaways. Throughout the extensive and well-tended grounds sit numerous small buildings connected by meandering secluded paths.

In 1989, Forbes held his seventieth birthday party at the Mendoub. Flown in on private jets at Forbes's expense were—so the story goes—some eight hundred Hollywood stars,

Interior of the Forbes
Museum, 1991.   2 Walter Harris, *Morocco That Was*, 81.

U.S. statesmen, TV personalities, industrialists, and publishing barons, Elizabeth Taylor and Henry Kissinger among them. The celebration, during which hundreds of musicians, acrobats, and Berber horsemen entertained the guests, apparently cost $2.5 million. Forbes died the following year. Soon after, the palace was turned into the Forbes Museum of Military Miniatures to display his impressive collection of toy soldiers. At the time of writing, 2006, it is closed, and its future is uncertain.

Not all of the palace was open to visitors, but the portion that was accessible gave a superb idea of how the rich lived in Tangier. Each window opened onto a different vista: of a vine-laden trellis, a tiled courtyard with a bubbling fountain, or the limitless horizon of the Atlantic Ocean. Immense, airy rooms with high ceilings were cooled by ocean breezes. The grounds, too, were open, and a peaceful day could be had dreaming on a terrace or in a hidden gazebo.

I went to gawk at the house but ended up even more fascinated by the collection. In room after room, glass display cases were filled with thousands of soldiers set up in war formation, re-creating such conflicts as the Green March of 1975, when Morocco sent settlers to the Spanish Sahara, skirmishes of the 1870–71 Franco-Prussian War, and the Battle of Trafalgar.

Forbes's ashes are on a Fijian island, but Walter Harris lies in the graveyard at St Andrew's, Tangier's Anglican church. Mustapha, the aged caretaker, proudly shows visitors around the small church, pointing out its Moorish arches, as well as the graves of Harris and others. From the grounds of the church, you can see the Grand Hôtel Villa de France, where Matisse stayed. In 1991, it was still possible to share this splendid though faded place with discreet Tangerine prostitutes and their clients. The views from most rooms—of the hotel's garden, the medina farther on, and the distant port—were magnificent.

By 1993 the Villa de France was closed, slated for redevelopment. Our hopes to stay there again were dashed, but we had noticed a pension just around the corner, in a grand two-story house with beautiful grounds. The caretaker of the Villa de France shrugged his shoulders when asked if that would be a good alternative. "What place could be as good as this?" he asked sadly.

We checked into the pension, a former residence of *The grounds of the* a European diplomat, judging from its position in the *Grand Hôtel Villa de* embassy quarter. The reception clerk asked for pay- *France, 1991.* ment in advance, an odd request in Tangier. This request and the unusual number of vivacious young women hanging about in housecoats—were they using the hotel as a dorm while they attended college?—should have warned us of the evening activities to come: an endless stream of Mercedes Benzes pulling up in the driveway to be greeted by the college-aged girls, now even more vivacious in their slinky dresses.

There are a number of confectionary shops, selling candies
and dried fruits — plums, dates, apricots, some sugared, some
But these shops also sell a confection of a different sort — drie
sugared (?) fish and candied (?) snake (?) squid

sesamed

fish look
sort of like
this + flat
brown colours.
Snake (?) bits
are golden colour
and worny looking

One place (one of many) is the

HUI LUO COPNT IFINHITE CTTINKFT S

The No 1 Department Store on Nanjing Donglu at Xizang Zhonglu
is a riot — the ladies wear section on the 2nd floor has racks
clothing with clerks standing nearby, wearing the same
outfit. It's disorienting
at first, then
hilarious. I
couldn't keep
a straight face.

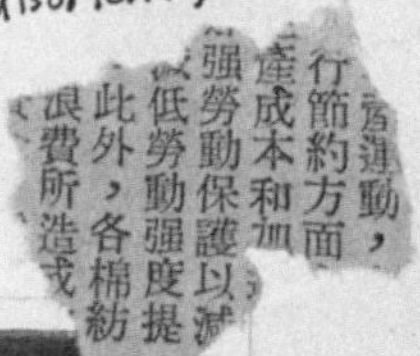

强劳动
达成本和加
行简约方面
为进动，
此外，各棉纺
限费所，造成
低劳动强度提
保护以减

No. 1
Department
Store

上海市第一百货商店股份有限公司
发票联——11
3100441322 0369
发票专用章

购货单位
货   号
商品名

二0b

合计人民币 (大写)

本发票须加盖收讫章有效

Bought more labels
here because a package
was only 2.5 ¥ — so
bought 2 for 5. Receipt
Old fashioned take →
slip to cashier, pays, take
stamped slip back to counter,
pick up item.

工商登记号 150066600
国税沪字第 31004413220 3694

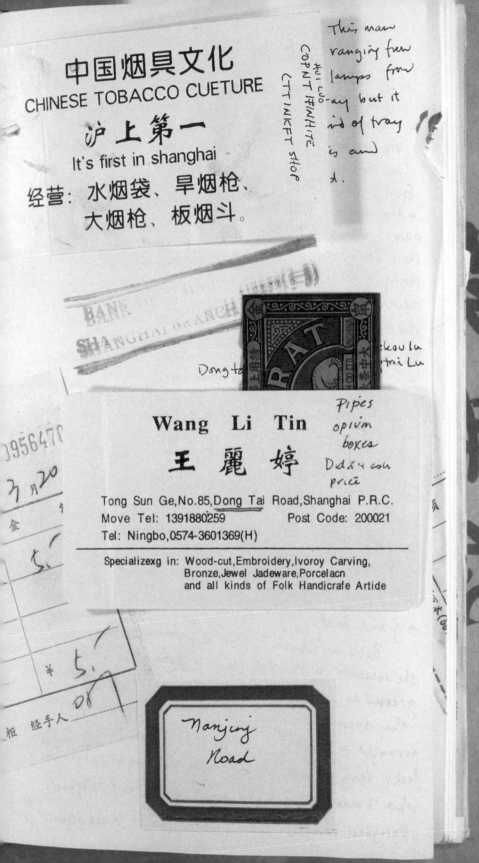

中国烟具文化
CHINESE TOBACCO CUETURE

沪上第一
It's first in shanghai

经营：水烟袋、旱烟枪、
大烟枪、板烟斗。

This man ranging from lamps from -ay but it ind of tray is and t.

HUI LUO
COPNT HANHITE
CTTINKFT SHOP

BANK
SHANGHAI BRANCH

Dong ta

RAT

ckou lu
ntai Lu

Wang   Li   Tin

王 麗 婷

Pipes
opium
boxes
Didn't ash
price

Tong Sun Ge, No. 85, Dong Tai Road, Shanghai P.R.C.
Move Tel: 1391880259   Post Code: 200021
Tel: Ningbo, 0574-3601369(H)

Specializexg in: Wood-cut, Embroidery, Ivoroy Carving,
Bronze, Jewel Jadeware, Porcelacn
and all kinds of Folk Handicrafe Artide

Nanjing
Road

Shopping on a Grand Scale

SHANGHAI

DEPARTMENT STORES IN CHINA ARE MUCH LIKE THOSE in North America. They are large—generally five or six stories, covering much of a city block. They sell what department stores around the world sell. They have escalators and sales clerks, and the prices are fixed. In the midst of all of these similarities, the differences become bewildering and endearing.

In Tientsin's International Market Department Store, for example, a sales clerk—there are far more of them than of customers, and none appears to be over the age of nineteen—wolfs down a bowl of noodles while crouching behind a folding room divider.

Beijing's Hongqiao Market on Tiantan Street, close to the Temple of Heaven, seems to be a department store with its postmodern brass and glass exterior. But the ground-floor doors open onto a fish market, where several dozen rubber-booted fishmongers are shouting, spraying water, and slapping their fish onto tables. The fish give way to heaps of vegetables and fruits. Countertops display slender boxes decorated with elegant gilt calligraphy. Inside each is a carefully chosen gnarly tuber guaranteed to provide vigor and long life. On the next floor are stalls and tables where watches and clocks are sold, and on the next are leather bags, CDs, shoes, suits, and sweaters. It becomes apparent that this is not an emporium run by one merchant but a genuine market with hundreds of vendors. The third floor contains a pearl market, with some forty or fifty dealers who will make you a necklace on the spot, and an antique market, a somewhat rarefied warren of small rooms filled with Mao memorabilia, jade vases, snuff bottles, and silks.

Although the antiques were what I had come for, I became mesmerized by the pearl market and spent an afternoon sitting first with one vendor, then with another, listening to the Russian, English, Mandarin,

FACING PAGE: *Matchbox covers found in Shanghai.*

PREVIOUS SPREAD: *Notes made after a walk up Nanking Road (Nanjing Dong Lu).*

The Wing On Co., Ltd. Shanghai Building 上海永安有限公司自建洋樓

and German of the buyers and watching the intricate negotiations of the wholesale jewelry trade. A man with a monocular glass screwed into his eye is intent on picking out perfection; a bleached blonde with long, painted nails avidly sorts through gold and lapis lazuli, pointedly ignoring her bored husband.

In Shanghai, department stores have been developed to a high art; there you will even find a Printemps, seemingly transplanted straight from Paris, and an Itokin, similarly transported direct from Tokyo.[1]

The venerable No. 1 Department Store on Nanjing Dong Lu (formerly Nanking Road) opened in 1934 as the Sun Department Store, one of four grand emporiums built around the same time; the others are the Wing On, the Sincere, and the Sun Sun department stores.

The No. 1 is especially charming with its wintertime displays of thick, flesh-colored support-hose stockings on upturned mannequin legs. But the dress department is one of my most vivid memories of Shanghai. At the time of my visit, in 1999, this department was filled with racks, each hung with dresses of the same style and color. At the

---

1 In stark contrast to the overstuffed feel of many Chinese department stores, the Itokin is elegantly understocked. Refolding the six sweaters in the sporting department or repositioning the six toy cars in the men's accessories section does not give the staff much to do, so they concentrate on greeting customers. During the course of several ascents by escalator to the eighth floor Chalon Restaurant, my companion and I swore we heard the clerks on each floor call out a pleasant "Good morning," even though we were never there before 7:30 PM.

end of each rack stood a mannequin wearing that same style of dress. One expected her to be made of plastic, but instead, she was alive. To see the first mannequin turn her head to watch your approach was to skip a heartbeat. To see dozens of such young women, each dressed to match the clothes on the rack she stood next to, was a surrealistic experience surely unmatched in any department store anywhere else in the world.

Because Chinese department stores are so idiosyncratic, shopping—or at least window-shopping—in them does not seem to betray any loftier goals, such as experiencing the more intimate aspects of a city. That said, however, the small stores are irresistible.

Those who have read up on Shanghai's history will look askance at the many calligraphy supply shops along the city's Fuzhou Lu (Foochow Road), knowing they have replaced the untold numbers of brothels, gambling joints, and opium dens that lined the street in the 1920s and '30s.

Along Nanjing Dong Lu, specialty shops sell an array of foodstuffs. One such store calls itself the Hui Luo Copnt Ifinhite Cttinkft Shop. At these places, sweets and preserved fruit are displayed alongside tiny, flat dried fish and shrimps and king-size seahorses; the juxtaposition is disconcerting. The

temptation to bring back samples was tempered by the devastating odors, and in any case, these particular tidbits can be found in Chinatowns throughout North America and Europe.

Even window-shopping at the Shanghainese restaurants is an experience. Where else can you see blue-faced frogs—seemingly made out of porcelain until they inflate their bladder-like cheeks—that weigh four pounds if they weigh an ounce? If ornamental amphibians do not destroy your appetite, the descriptions on the menu will: braised sea slug, fried croaker in sweet sour sauce, sautéed river eel with five treasures, cup of crocodile claw, steamed ovaducts, gall bladder, and duck tongue in hot oil, to name a few. I made a point of inventorying Shanghai's vast array of foods that I had never dreamed of eating. Each restaurant window became a magnet. Would the snakes be longer, fatter, in this one? What does crocodile claw look like? When is that mound of black, slimy stuff going to start moving?

The numerous antique markets are far more appealing—the Fuyou Lu, the Huabao Building, and the Dongtai being among the most established. Of them, the Fuyou Lu Sunday Market could provide the sole reason for visiting Shanghai. Despite its name, it is open daily. Once a street market, it is now located in the Cang Bao Antiques Building at 457 Fangbang Zhonglu. The main floor is the

most organized and official, with vendors selling from stalls. On the next two floors, wares are spread out on tables, and on the top floor, the vendors, who are harder up, sell off the floor.

ABOVE: *A Shanghai food market, c. 1930.*

NEXT SPREAD: *Photographs from Shanghai's Fuyou Lu Market.*

For the earnest collector, the middle two floors are the most promising. My successes included matchbox cover proofs glued onto yellowed newspapers, as well as old photographs and identity cards. Word of my interest in photographs spread quickly among the dealers, and I was soon approached by elderly women holding up stacks of studio portraits and boys offering envelopes bursting with snapshots. A young man came up to me with an album that had been assembled by a French family in the 1930s. "How much is this?" I asked him, flipping through the pages plastered with photos taken at the racetrack, by the swimming pool, on the Bund.

"One hundred American dollars," he replied, quite breathless.

"Oh, that's too much," I protested, as I continued to peruse this treasure.

"But it's not for sale," he said. "I just bought it, and I *knew* you'd be interested to see it." We agreed that it was a lot of money, but for him, even though the cost must have been even more prohibitive than for me, possessing this glimpse into his city's past was worth it.

The Great World

JOSEF VON STERNBERG, THE DIRECTOR OF SUCH coolly impassioned movies as *The Shanghai Express* and *The Shanghai Gesture*, spent time in Shanghai during the height of the city's cosmopolitan years, just before the Japanese invasion of China in 1937.

In the 1930s, the population of Shanghai was drawn from every part of the world—or, rather, the "underworld." White Russians controlled the brothels, a Jewish merchant from Baghdad had cornered the opium trade, nearly every nationality was represented in the vast network of spies, reporting to at least six governments: Chinese, French, English, German, American, and Japanese.

Mary Pickford and Douglas Fairbanks, Noël Coward, Count Galeazzo Ciano (Mussolini's son-in-law), Wallis Simpson, André Malraux, Charlie Chaplin, and Eugene O'Neill (in disguise as Reverend William O'Brian and on the mend from a nervous breakdown), were just a few of the celebrities who hung out in Shanghai, looking for action at the Cathay Hotel, the Cercle Sportif Français, the Canidrome, or the Race Course.

Many of these decadent places are gone or altered beyond recognition, but one survives more or less intact: the Great World Entertainment Complex, also known as the Da Shi Jie Arcadia and the Shanghai Youth Palace (a remnant from the Communist period). It was the description in Sternberg's autobiography, *Fun in a Chinese Laundry*, that convinced me a visit there would be worthwhile. In Sternberg's time, the Great World was owned by a Huang Chujiu, who had made his fortune selling a brain-toning elixir, among other pharmaceuticals. When he lost his money, the complex came into the hands of Huang "Pockmarked"

ABOVE: *A luggage label for Shanghai's Cathay Hotel.*

FACING PAGE: *Shanghai by night with the admission ticket for the Great World Entertainment Complex.*

Jinrong, a notorious Shanghai crime boss and a former officer in the French gendarmerie.

The Great World has been located at the intersection of Yunan Lu and Xizang Lu (the former Avenue Edward the Seventh and Tibet Road) since it first opened in 1917. According to many sources, it survived the sixty-some years from the Japanese occupation to the war against Japan to the Revolution and finally to the reforms following Communism, for the most part hanging on to its purpose as a place to go have fun. According to Sternberg, however, it was bombed by the Chinese themselves and destroyed.

Whether we were visiting the original Great World or a reincarnation of it, I did not care. It was enough that it had the same name and stood in the same location. My companion and I timed our 8:45 PM arrival to coincide with what I figured would be the start of the real action. The entrance, as in many Chinese buildings, was poorly lit, enhancing the illicit nature of the place. We bought our tickets for thirteen yuan each (around $2.50) and followed the signs to the Hall of Mirrors. The distorted reflections and the low lighting immediately recalled that other Shanghai-titled movie, Orson Welles's *The Lady from Shanghai*. The effect was dampened by the only other person in the room, a skinny sweeper. Clearly, if anything was about to happen, it was going to be closing time, not a wild and hallucinogenic shoot-out.

We hastened along, afraid that we'd be whisked to the exit and miss whatever spectacles remained. Sternberg wrote that there were six floors and that the higher up you went, the more perverse the entertainment became. He described gambling, sing-song girls, magicians, acrobats, extractors of earwax, stuffed curiosities, story-tellers, and more girls, these with dresses "slit up to their armpits." Still on the main floor, we discovered a bumper car attraction. Then we came to a stage featuring young jugglers and contortionist acrobats. They performed flawlessly and with much vigor before the handful of spectators. This is more like it, I thought, and we sat a while to watch them.

We then climbed the stairs and continued to watch the acrobats from the second-floor walkway, but the promise of more excitement

A Chinese actor, c. 1910.

tempted us to further exploration, which revealed a video arcade, a restaurant, and snack bars. An opera performance in a small theater was obscured by thick tobacco smoke as the audience furiously puffed away at cigarettes. We reached the fourth or fifth floor—I lost track—and could go no farther. According to legend, those who made it to the top (the perhaps mythical sixth floor), having lost all of their money, jumped off. That the suicides have gone the way of the sing-song girls is no doubt a good thing. In the end, we left before the doors closed for the night.

My visit to the Great World, oddly enough, did not destroy any of my notions of how it would be; rather, it created a continuity from Sternberg's vivid description of the place at its most exuberant to the odd and dilapidated place it had become.

Arrivals

STANLEY

THE MOST COVETED OF ALL FALKLAND Island souvenirs is something forbidden. It mustn't be touched; even approaching it may prove fatal. The tourist who does manage to procure one and gets caught leaving the country with it faces imprisonment and a heavy fine. This prohibited item is the minefield warning plaque found on fences and posts all over the Falklands but mainly on East Falkland, where the capital, Stanley, is located. It never occurred to me that these signs existed, let alone that people might remove them, until February 2000, when I arrived at the island's Mount Pleasant Airport on a flight from Santiago, Chile.

We disembarked and walked across the tarmac in the cold wind of a gray mid-autumn day and entered the arrivals hall, a small, bare room with a stationary luggage carousel in the middle. The line to have passports stamped formed immediately. It is necessary to have a visa to visit the Falklands, but visas are not hard to obtain. One of the main requirements is that you have a return ticket and that you arrange your accommodation before arrival. Nonetheless, a Yugoslavian in the queue who proposed to camp and showed the customs agent his pup tent was admitted.

Suddenly we heard a loud thud. A military officer dressed in green had jumped up onto the luggage carousel and was demanding our attention. If my memory serves me correctly, he wore a tam and a heavy sweater reinforced at the elbows with patches. What really drew our attention was the notice board he held and the particularly military way he shouted, "Right!"

ABOVE AND FACING:
Souvenirs from the
Falkland Islands—
petrel feathers and a
sketch of wild bird eggs.

DECLINATION—*same Name as*—LATITUDE.

	12°	13°	14°	15°	16°	17°	18°	19°	20°	21°	22°	23°
	° ′	° ′	° ′	° ′	° ′	° ′	° ′	° ′	° ′	° ′	° ′	° ′
	82 42	82 5	81 28	80 50	80 12	79 34	78 56	78 17	77 38	76 59	76 20	75 4
	81 55	81 18	80 41	80 3	79 25	78 47	78 9	77 31	76 52	76 13	75 34	74 5
	81 8	80 31	79 54	79 16	78 39	78 1	77 23	76 45	76 7	75 28	74 49	74 1
	80 21	79 44	79 7	78 30	77 53	77 15	76 37	76 0	75 22	74 43	74 4	73 2
	79 34	78 57	78 20	77 43	77 6	76 28	75 51	75 14	74 36	73 57	73 19	72 4
	78 47	78 10	77 33	76 56	76 19	75 42	75 5	74 28	73 50	73 12	72 34	71 5
	78 0	77 23	76 47	76 10	75 33	74 56	74 19	73 42	73 5	72 27	71 49	71 1
	77 13	76 36	76 0	75 23	74 46	74 9	73 33	72 56	72 19	71 41	71 4	70 2
	76 26	75 49	75 13	74 36	74 0	73 23	72 47	72 10	71 33	70 55	70 18	69 4
	75 38	75 2	74 26	73 50	73 14	72 37	72 1	71 25	70 48	70 10	69 33	68 5
	74 51	74 15	73 39	73 3	72 27	71 50	71 15	70 39	70 2	69 24	68 48	68 1
	74 3	73 28	72 52	72 16	71 40	71 4	70 29	69 53	69 16	68 39	68 3	67 2
	73 16	72 41	72 5	71 29	70 53	70 18	69 43	69 7	68 31	67 54	67 18	66 4
	72 29	71 54	71 18	70 42	70 6	69 31	68 56	68 21	67 45	67 8	66 32	65 5
	71 41	71 7	70 31	69 55	69 20	68 45	68 10	67 35	66 59	66 22	65 47	65 1
	70 54	70 20	69 44	69 8	68 34	67 59	67 24	66 49	66 13	65 37	65 2	64 2
	70 7	69 32	68 57	68 21	67 47	67 12	66 37	66 2	65 27	64 51	64 16	63 4
		68 44	68 9	67 33	66 59	66 25	65 5				63 30	62 5
			67 21	66 46	66 12						44	62
			66 34	65 58	65 24	64					58	61 2
	Sun rises 4h 54m sets 7h 6m bearg 69°47′	Sun rises 4h 49m sets 7h 11m bearg 68° 3′	65 11	64 37	64						12	60 3
			Sun rises 4h 43m sets 7h 17m bearg 66°17′	63 50	63						26	59 5
				63 2	62						40	59
				Sun rises 4h 37m sets 7h 23m bearg 64°32′	61						54	58 2
					Sun rises 4h 31m sets 7h 29m bearg 62°44′	Sun rises 4h 2? sets 7h 3? bearg 60°					8	57 3
											21	56 4
											34	56
											47	55 1
											0	54 2
											13	53 4
											26	52 5
											38	52
											51	51 2
								bearg 57°15′	rises 7h 56m sets 8h 2m bearg 55°22′	rises 8h 58m sets 8h 10m bearg 53°27′	Sun rises 8h 50m sets 8h 10m	50 3
												49 4
											Sun rises 3h 43m sets 8h 17m bearg 49° 3

1. *Pagodroma nivea*
2. *Larus dominicani*
3. *Procellaria aequin...*

I'm sure there were some inadvertent half salutes among the octogenarians in the crowd. Ramrod straight, the officer pointed to a picture on the board. "This is a land mine!" he barked. "Look carefully." His finger moved down to the next picture. "This is a minefield plaque! It warns you to stay away." There was a long list of dos and don'ts. "This is what you do if you find a land mine." He proceeded to describe the variety of unexploded devices—grenades, mortars, shells, rockets, bullets—waiting since the conflict of 1982 to explode and blow off our limbs. He told us not to touch any suspicious object, to mark the location (on our Ordnance maps, which we will not leave Stanley without), to place an indicator close by, to make a note of its characteristics, and to tell the Joint Service Explosive Ordnance Disposal Operations Centre (JSEODOC) or the police as soon as possible.

Then he became very serious. Those of us who had relaxed sprang back to attention. "Above all"—he seemed to be looking each of us future perpetrators in the eye—"DO NOT REMOVE THE SIGNS. Anyone caught doing so will be punished to the full extent of the law. Do not think you will be able to leave the island with one. X-ray machines will be used on every piece of luggage, and all metal will be examined."

I may have a few of his words wrong, but that was the tenor. Mess with land-mine plaques, and you mess with him or one of his lot. As a result, land mines fascinated me for the entire trip, and it was to my great disappointment that I saw only one plaque and that was from the safety of a moving vehicle. The islands I visited—Sea Lion, Carcass, and Saunders—were land mine free. My forays in the environs of Stanley were not adventurous.

I questioned Falklanders about the land mines. How many people have been blown up since 1982, I wanted to know. No one could say; it didn't seem to be an issue. How about penguins? They wander all over and don't read. Possible penguin deaths from mines were dismissed; the birds are apparently too light to set off the mines. Someone mentioned that he'd heard of the occasional sheep blowing up,

but there are many sheep on the Falklands, more than they need.

I limited my souvenirs to photographs and sketches, printed things like maps and souvenir booklets, and organic specimens such as ferns, lichen, mosses, tussock grass, shells, and feathers. Even then, as I approached the X-ray machine on the day of departure, it was with some trepidation. What if I had missed the part that said you could not remove *Fissurella picta*, the limpet shells that heavily coat the beaches? What if it was a crime to transport petrel down? My bags cleared the X-ray machine without a hitch; all of that anxiety had been for nothing.

Gentoo penguins on Sea Lion Island with nothing to fear.

A Natural History Boutique

IN 1998, I VISITED THE SANTA Monica outlet of an upscale clothing and household décor boutique chain that had evidently hired a brilliant buyer to bring in a variety of very odd stuff. At the time of my visit, the store stocked a selection of zoological and botanical specimen bottles and boxes, discards from an unnamed British museum. The bottles were labeled, and many contained intriguing residue. The boxes were of cardboard and glass; most were labeled, but all were empty. If chosen carefully, the boxes could be nested and thus were the easiest to transport. To my everlasting regret, I could only manage five and lacked the foresight to arrange to have more shipped home.

Other tempting items on offer included framed pressed plants, either truly vintage or convincingly done up to look so; blank books from India with lusciously thick paper and heavy leather bindings; and rusty, barely functional gardening tools. The store was a revelation, a marvel of daring eclecticism. There were other goods as well: mainly rattan furniture, home-style bed linens, and gypsy-style clothing of the sort found in more run-of-the-mill import stores.

The backs of the specimen boxes found in Los Angeles were as interesting as the fronts. This one has been augmented with a photograph and a parallel ruler, other L.A. finds.

By the following year, the specimen boxes and bottles were gone, snapped up by appreciative customers. They had been replaced by stacks of old French postal boxes, perfect for storing small envelopes. A highly anticipated visit in 2001 was a disappointment, however. The unusual imports had been supplanted by the mass-produced knickknacks found everywhere else. What had happened to that brilliant buyer?

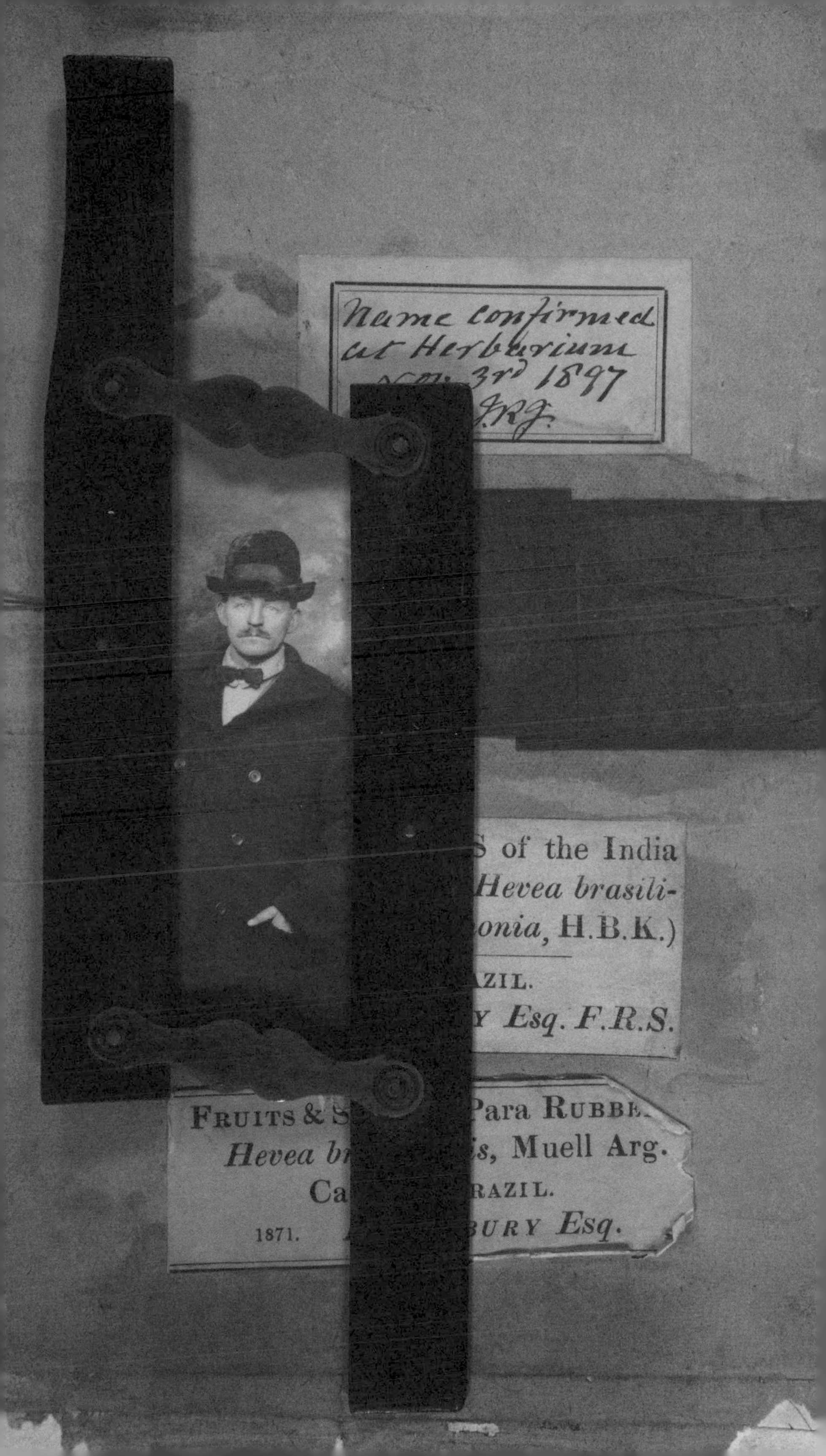

Name confirmed
at Herbarium
Nov. 3rd 1897
J.R.J.

...S of the India
...Hevea brasili-
...onia, H.B.K.)
...AZIL.
...y Esq. F.R.S.

FRUITS & S... Para Rubbe...
Hevea br... is, Muell Arg.
Ca... RAZIL.
1871. ...BURY Esq.

I'm not sure how I managed to find out about that store yet took so long to discover the Los Angeles-area flea markets. With its year-round reliable weather, Los Angeles is a perfect city for this type of Sunday pastime. Every weekend of every month, there is a flea market in Pasadena, Long Beach, Santa Monica, or Ventura. The goods on offer are similar to those in cities like Vancouver and Portland, but there is more, much more. And among the usual castoffs—the accordions, the typewriters, the lava lamps—lurk unexpected treasures.

What is it besides the weather that makes Los Angeles such a flea-marketer's heaven? Is it the large population, the presence of much wealth, the transience, or the enthusiasm to sell just about anything? Where else in the world can you buy a coffin at an outdoor market? I saw one for sale at the Roadium Open-Air Market in Torrance, en route to Long Beach. The vendor had tucked his business cards behind the pristine brass plaque *(Your name here!)*, then absented himself, confident that no one would make off with his merchandise.

Long Beach Outdoor Market, established in 1982, sets up at the Veterans Stadium. On the third Sunday of the month, eight hundred dealers hawk their wares; on specially scheduled Sundays, if there is an extra weekend in the month, as few as six hundred may show up. Because it is entirely outdoors, unlike markets in Vancouver or Portland, the place has a festive air, ideal for sunbathing, eating hot dogs, tossing a Frisbee. But it's only open from eight until three, so there's no time to waste.

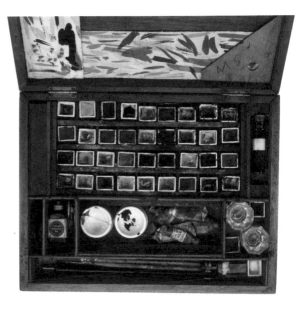

The dealers here haggle good-naturedly; they enjoy explaining the history behind what they are selling. People making the rounds are also an amiable lot and, in that wonderful American tradition of friendliness and openness, think nothing of inspecting your purchase and asking what you paid for it and what you plan to do with it.

I visited Long Beach with a friend, an habituée of Los Angeles flea markets. At first we were wary of each other's company. Flea marketing with a new partner can be a disappointing experience. She is too slow, he talks too much, she turns up her nose at the things you are interested in, he wants you to get excited about the trash he likes. My companion was perfect. Moving efficiently from stall to stall, eyes sharp for what she wanted and for what I was seeking as well, and friendly with the dealers, she was also a dab hand at negotiation. We moved along at a matching pace and finished up pretty much at the same time.

I found a small tin set of watercolors, a children's book about the circus (see next page), and a Turkish harem doll (shown opposite). My friend came away with an identification badge for a wartime airplane mechanic, a blanket printed with sailboats for a boating friend, and photographs. Thanks to her indefatigable demands on my behalf for paint sets in wooden boxes, I later ended up with a gorgeous example (pictured above) that belonged to a vendor who knew he had one "somewhere" and actually went home and found it.

As for the boutique chain, I no longer haunt its aisles, vainly hoping to find something of interest. With so many other more interesting choices, who needs to?

CIRCUS SPORTS

The Measure of the Criminal

I FOUND THE PIECE OF PAPER PICTURED OPPOSITE IN A BINDER at an ephemera market in Portland, Oregon. It concerns a fellow named George Davis, who lived sometime in the early twentieth century and who would have remained anonymous if he hadn't been a crook. Because of his antisocial occupation, he became a wanted man, and his mug shot was sent from Portland to police stations all over the United States.

Davis had two aliases: John H. Gavin and W. J. Morrison. The Portland police also called him #1476. His portrait, shown full face and in profile, could be that of a farmer, a laborer, a mechanic, a bank robber. You look at him and think he has posed for pictures like this before, in another town, maybe, for another charge. He knows the ropes; he's completely nonchalant. Then you look again and change your mind: he is down on his luck; he has never done this before; he does not know that he needs to worry, to look ashamed.

Davis was twenty-six years old when the circular was published. How old did you think he was? Thirty, perhaps? I thought that he was around thirty-five. What kind of life did he lead to look so old? He was only 5 feet 7½ inches tall and stooped as well, and he weighed a scant 123 pounds. I would not have thought him a hefty man, but he looks deceptively larger in his photograph. That he had brown hair is evident. His blue eyes are harder to distinguish, as the sepia tone deludes. He apparently had some scarring around his fingers and his knees, nothing we would notice if we had met him on the street.

The circular gives a series of numbers: 70.5–73.0–94.3–18.8–15.6–14.5–6.2–25.0–11.2–8.6–45.2, labeled a Bertillon description.

Police Headquarters
(Detective Department)

Circular #71   Portland, Ore.

Chief of Police,

Dear Sir;

    Enclosed fine Photo and Bertillon
Geo. Da͟vis, alias John H. Gavin, alias
whom we hold warrant for Grand Larceny,
7½ in., 123#, brown hair, blue eyes, lig
a little stooped,

    Bertillon; 70.5--73.0--94.3--18.
5.2--25.0--11.2--8.6--45.2

    Finger print Classification; $\dfrac{25 \quad 0 \quad 19}{24 \quad I}$

    Vertical scar ½" long at second joint right little
finger,   Vertical scar 1" long at 2" below right knee;
small round scar at right knee; Small round scar 3" below
right knee.

    e are very anxious to apprehend this man and would
ppreciate any effort you would make toward this end. If
ound arrest, hold and wire us and we will arrange to have
im returned to this city at once.

        Yours truly,

            B. A. Slover,
                Acting Chief of Police,

            C. B. Baty,
                Captain of Detectives.

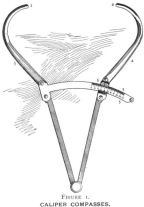

FIGURE 1.
CALIPER COMPASSES.

A set of calipers for
measuring the breadth
of the head. From
Alphonse Bertillon's
Instructions for Taking
Descriptions for the
Identification of
Criminals and Others
by the means of
Anthropometric
Indications *(Chicago:*
American Bertillon
Prison Bureau, 1889).

This numbering system was created by Alphonse Bertillon, a Frenchman, to help police distinguish a man like Davis from every other man with a similar appearance, to ensure, as it were, that they got the right man in their nationwide search for him.

Bertillon worked as a clerk for the police in Paris. In 1882 he managed to convince his superiors that his system of measurements, along with the side-by-side front-and-profile portraits, were useful in identifying known criminals. The system was adopted, and the filing cabinets soon bulged with head shots and measurements and no efficient means to retrieve the information. Nonetheless, police departments around the world noticed this method of quantifying the criminal, which came to be called Bertillonage. It was adopted in the United States around 1887.

How often Bertillonage failed isn't known, but after 1903, when a man who fit the Bertillon description for a wanted criminal was arrested and proved to be innocent, its use declined and was replaced by fingerprint comparison. Davis was identified by both Bertillon and fingerprints.

So, what do the numbers 70.5–73.0–94.3–18.8–15.6–14.5–6.2–25.0–11.2–8.6–45.2 tell us? The figure 18.8, for example, was his head length, measured in centimeters; 6.2 cm was his right-ear height and 25 cm his foot length (corresponding roughly to ladies' size nine). These and other key features were measured with either a pair of Bertillon calipers or a set of sliding compasses. Davis's measurements confirm that he was on the small side but add nothing much else to our picture of him.

Wanted notices are fascinating on many levels. First there are the photographs. Because the subject is an alleged criminal, these portraits seem infinitely more revealing than ordinary portraits. Your expectations that the arrested person should look alarmed,

LOS ANGELES, CAL. Dec. 20th, 1906

ARREST FOR FORGERY, I HOLD WARRANT,

WALTER BRANCH, whose picture is shown here-
on. German descent, 23 years old; height 5 ft.
6 in., weight 148 lbs.; light brown eyes; brown
hair slightly curly; hair mole on right cheek.
Was wearing when last seen in this city, December
10th, 1906, a fairly good suit of gray mixed or
"pepper and salt" goods, and a soft brown hat.
Teamster. May drive express wagon.
HOLD AND NOTIFY

EDWARD KERN,
CHIEF OF POLICE.

despondent, or ashamed are often overturned, not by a jolly, smiling
face, but by one that is possibly indifferent, more likely confident
or cocky.

Then there is the personal information. One early mug shot in my
possession details the usual weight, height, and coloring of a Walter
Branch (shown above), then describes his "fairly good suit of gray
mixed or 'pepper and salt' goods, and a soft brown hat" and adds
that he "may drive an express wagon." Walter, by the way, was
photographed in profile by means of a mirror.

By the 1940s, the circulars had become more uniform and more
detailed. Names of relatives appeared, along with addresses, number
of children, previous convictions, and religion, as well as drinking,
smoking, and narcotics habits. The arresting officer filled in
preprinted blanks rather than composing his own narrative.

Most of the mug shots that I own were acquired in Portland, the
originating city of the circular for George Davis. Other cities represented in my Portland finds include Los Angeles, California;

Lansing, Kansas; Walla Walla, Washington; and Great Falls, Montana. The abundance of these portraits in Portland is probably due to the fact that the city hosts several major collectible and paper ephemera shows each year, attracting dealers from all over the United States and Canada. If I attended such shows in other cities, I would probably find selections just as good. But for me, Portland will always be the capital of the criminal mug shot.

How much of one thing does one really need? This is a good question to address while we are still in Portland, for this city not only hosts the aforementioned ephemera shows but also has three annual large antique and collectibles fairs. They are held in the Metropolitan Exposition Center at the northern edge of the city. In the fall and spring, the 1,350 vendors are confined to three large halls; in the summer, the number swells to around eighteen hundred and they spill out into the parking lot. There are larger shows in the United States (the Pasadena Rose Bowl has over two thousand *every month*), but this one will do just fine.

Collecting often begins innocently. Many people start with a single item that somehow found its way into their home: a birthday present, an inheritance, perhaps. Then one day, they spot another, similar item and think that two would look twice as interesting as one. Suddenly, they have a collection; they buy another, then another. Before they know it, every waking moment is spent adding to it. Their searches are usually regulated: by price, by color or size, by originality. The more avid of these collectors sometimes find that they single-handedly drive up the cost of that particular item.

Others decorate their homes in a certain style—Art Deco, retro '40s, and Stickley come to mind—and buy complementary items. There is danger here. Not only do such people amass large items such as beds, sofas, even staircases, but their collection can be unbalanced by the smallest acquisition outside of the style and take them in whole new directions.

Still others have no theme or goal or vision. They are the magpies of the business, picking up anything for any reason, especially if someone else wants it. Such collectors also have difficulties throwing anything out and have crammed houses and apartments with everything from empty pop bottles to gramophones to copies of *Look* magazine. Despairing parents or spouses cajole, nag, even berate the collector to clean up, to organize, to sell, or at least to clear a path.

Too much of a good thing, or not enough? These cigarette boxes are a mere dip into the obsession known as tobacciana, the collection of smoking artifacts.

The last main category of collectors are those seeking the Aladdin's lamp of antiques, the sensational find that will make them a fortune and send anxious ripples through the antiquarian world, compelling everyone to look more closely at that grimy oil painting or box of jewels tucked away in the attic. With bookshelves groaning under the weight of reference material, a calculator always within reach, and a cell phone at hand to transmit photos and details instantly, these are the collectors to learn from. After all, you can't go on wasting money on trash forever. Or can you?

Dr Wilsone's Fossils

VANCOUVER

VANCOUVER WAS FOUNDED IN THE 1880s, so its homegrown material wealth is relatively recent and unremarkable. The city has never had much of an industry in creating fine objects, whether furniture, porcelains, textiles, or other sought-after products, and, aside from being a notable source of Northwest Coast Native art, the arts and crafts here are young, especially compared with Europe or Asia. Local antiques are of the twentieth-century kind: workaday china, roughly constructed pine furniture and folk art, prints of sentimental scenes, biscuit tins (usually the worse for wear), 1940s office furniture of stainless steel and leatherette, and builders' tools of all kinds.

Unlike France, Britain, Holland, or Germany, where objects from their respective colonies can be found in specialty shops, Canada itself was a colony. Moreover, many settlers brought little of value from the Old Country, aside from personal memorabilia; most of them started fresh once they arrived. When souvenirs of foreign travel appear, it is by chance: an estate giving up its secret collections or an entrepreneur hoping to add a spark to the shopping scene.

Nevertheless, I am continually surprised and delighted by what turns up. An inlaid table from Damascus via Fiesole, an ivory miniature of the nineteenth-century traveler Jane Digby, a coppered tin samovar from Kashmir, opium pipes from China, saddle frames and blankets from the Near East, an Indian dancer's Mogul-style jackets and vests, hand-colored engravings from Maria Sybilla Merian's

ABOVE: *Microscope slides found at a Vancouver market housed in a salvaged box.*

FACING PAGE: *Minerals, fossils, and shells from America, 1836. A portion of a collection assembled by Dr Wilsone.*

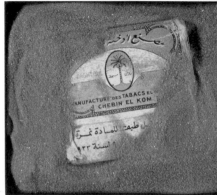

LEFT: *Fossil limestone from near the base of the Cheops Pyramid, looking towards the Great Pyramid, Gizeh, 1836.*

RIGHT: *Cigarette carton from the sands near the Great Pyramid, Gizeh, 1996.*

Metamorphosis Insectorum Surinamensium, 1726, and from d'Urville's *Voyage de la corvette l'Astrolabe*, 1833, are a few of the diverse treasures I have found here. The flea markets are one source; auctions are even better.

Much of what I look for is dictated by the projects I am working on. At particular times, I've been searching for ephemera from Morocco, for anatomical engravings from Austria and Hungary, for maps of the South Atlantic, for house plans from Damascus, for pulp novels about opium addiction or Western women escaping to harems. It would be ideal always to be prepared, always to know in advance what will be needed, but there are occasions when I cannot resist the object itself, if only for its history. Take the following example.

In 1836 and 1837, a Dr D. H. Wilsone of Greenock, Scotland, visited the United States, Egypt, and Palestine. He toured extensively and applied himself—like many travelers of the time—to the study of natural history.

I know about Dr Wilsone because some of his minerals, shells, and fossils came up for sale. The seller was a Scot, now a Vancouver resident. The collection had been in her family for years, but their connection with Dr Wilsone had long been forgotten.

Crammed into two wooden boxes were some sixty specimens,

each numbered and cross-referenced to an incomplete catalog. Many were individually wrapped in worn scraps of newspaper dating from 1836 or 1837—the *Times of London*, the New York *Observer*, for example. Others had been rewrapped in papers from the 1870s, 1890s, or 1940s. Folded around the first rock that I examined was the *Times* birth and death notices for 1836. I was astonished to read on this page of the death of Adalbert, the young son of Emmeline Stuart-Wortley, an Englishwoman whose fateful travels I had researched.

Many specimens were also given loose labels that listed relevant details in spidery, faded handwriting. The American examples included schist, gold ore, and marble, collected in the Rocky Mountains and at New York, Boston, Schuylkill, and Niagara Falls. Labels, such as that for a fragment of mica discolored by the Great Fire of New York, hinted at connections with past events.

As for the Egyptian and Palestinian materials, who could resist holding a fragment from Pompey's Pillar? Or a piece of "alabaster from the superb tomb of the Pacha"? Or shells gathered from the entrance to Cleopatra's Baths in Alexandria? Especially now, when to collect such items would rightfully be considered robbery.

What have I done with these stones and papers? Part of the collection went into temporary display in an exhibit of women travelers, as one example of the kinds of objects a nineteenth-century traveler might collect. The remaining specimens have become part of the re-creation of a cabinet of curiosities.

The Magnifying Glass

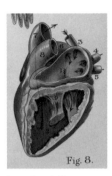

Fig. 8.

I HAVE FOUND SO MANY OBJECTS IN VANCOUVER that have been integral to my books that at times I wonder how I could have produced the books had I not lived here. My luck is partly due to my faithful attendance at the markets and partly to the random and bizarre way things turn up. I probably would have had similar luck in almost any other North American city, and possibly even better luck in Europe, but the following example shows how serendipitous a Vancouver flea market can be.

For my novel *The Sensualist*, set mainly in Vienna, I tried to find items related to anatomy and the history of medicine, especially with a German-language connection. I was encouraged by the discovery of some chromolithographs of pathological specimens printed in Leipzig but found in a cheap bin at a print seller's shop in London's Cecil Court. I purchased these for a couple of pounds, then started looking in earnest for other material. I soon realized that I had stumbled against a lofty and nearly impermeable circle, where my rivals were doctors with seemingly unlimited funding.

Booksellers specializing in anatomical treatises glanced at me with pity and sent me on my way. Dealers of antiquarian medical and scientific equipment at least allowed me to look at their unattainable wares. Slowly, painfully, I accumulated torn and stained prints, broken volumes, damaged vials. One of the things I desperately needed was something I didn't even know existed until I found it.

ABOVE AND FACING:
From Philips' Popular
Mannikin, *an anatomical
atlas, c. 1890.*

My novel mentioned a magnifying glass, but there was no point including a picture of one if it did not have some relevance to anatomy or medicine. On trips to Paris, Vienna, and Budapest, I had seen plenty of stylish magnifying glasses; there were even shops

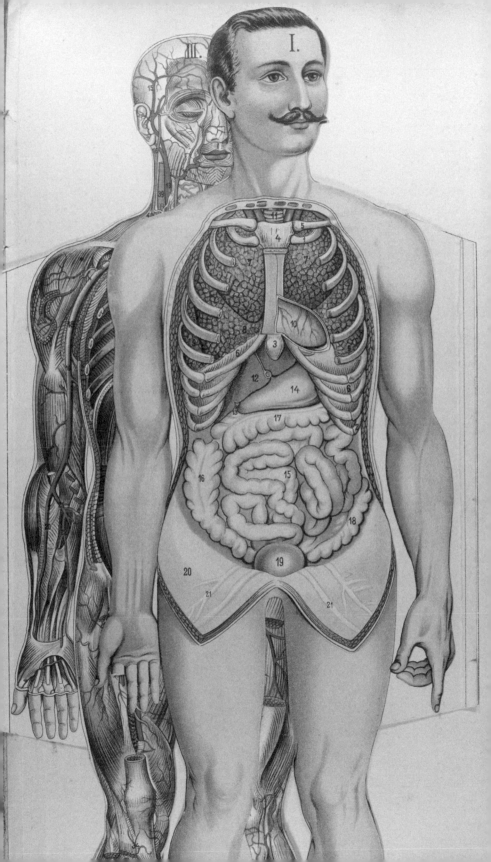

specializing in them, displaying models of varying ages, styles, strengths, and sizes. Handles were of ebony, ivory, bone, stag horn, or the lower leg and hoof of a gazelle. The glass, sometimes a subtle green or blue tint, was secured to the handles by frames made of sterling silver, brass, or steel. I had had no idea how sublime and exalted the art of the magnifying glass could be—or how expensive.

Finally, I gave up on the magnifying glass. One day, however, I accompanied a friend to a North Vancouver flea market (now gone) that occupied a dilapidated boatbuilding shed at the foot of Lonsdale Avenue, close to the harbor. This flea market was, frankly, a drag. It was poorly lit, cold, and depressing. Only collectors of plastic space figures or empty jam jars could find anything of interest there.

For some reason I thought about magnifying glasses. After passing several stalls, I stopped at one with a forlorn collection of kitchenware. I told the vendor that I wanted a magnifying glass. He replied that he had several. One was just what I could afford, only $1.50; the other was very expensive. I asked to see the cheap one, knowing I was just wasting my time. He produced a small glass with a yellow plastic rim. I shook my head. He shuffled some stuff around, commenting that the other one was way too much money, but he'd show it to me anyway. When he held it up, I could see that it was in another league entirely. The glass was powerful even at a distance, and the stainless steel rim was wide and had printing on it. I took it from him and inspected it closely. The words—some of which had been rubbed away by heavy use—were in German. Among them I could recognize words for parts of the body.

Two notable serendipitous Vancouver finds: the magnifying glass and a batch of documents from Galaţ, Romania, that included the passport of a woman who traveled in 1907. Shown here, from the same collection, is a mobilization order for a young man, dated 1891–99.

At moments like this, it is difficult to remain calm. I asked him how much too much money was. He thought for a moment and shook his head. Way too much. So, how much is way too much? He rubbed his jaw. Ten dollars, he replied. How had I the nerve to ask if he would take eight? But he accepted, and I became the owner of a 1920s or '30s German ophthalmologist's glass. A page in my book was waiting for it.

M? 76 N° 2644/91

Model No._____ din regulamentul de mobilisare.
și
Model No. 681 din nomenclatura imprimatelor.

DE ARMATĂ

Jandarm 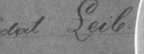 Galt

1) Regimentul Perel

RDIN·DE CHEMARE

No.

dat Leib.   destinat la 2)

eză că, în cas de m

N 11 Comp

torirea ca îndată ce,

că s'a ordonat mobilisar   ului căruia

rin en tul Perel N 11

nu va respunde la acestă chemare, se va trimit   judecată conform

odul just   militare, al căruî conținut se ara   contra-pagină.

ancul

Șeful de   ul de recrutare

pă saŭ serviciul în care comptéză omul.
ele și pronumele omuluï.
tatului decret No. 681 din 1898.
serviciul la care este destinat la mobilisare (de ex. regimentul 15 infanterie, cu   diviziei III, et
nde se mobiliséză corpul saŭ serviciul.
mnatura șefuluï de corp saŭ serviciuluï care trimite ordinul.
i sigiliŭ șefuluï deposituluï de recrutare.

sitele de recrutare vor înainta Ministerul de externe ordinele de chemare ale ómenilor domiciliă
oficiurï deschise, astfel ca Ministerul de externe să póta lua cunoștință de coprinsul lor.
onsulatele) înapoiază depositelor, prin Ministerul de externe, dovedile saŭ procesele-verbale (peut

B. 470. — Imprimeria Statulu

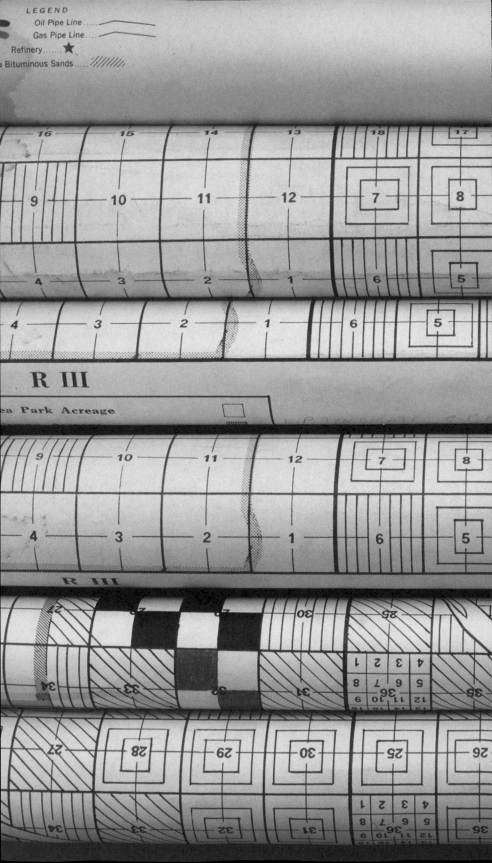

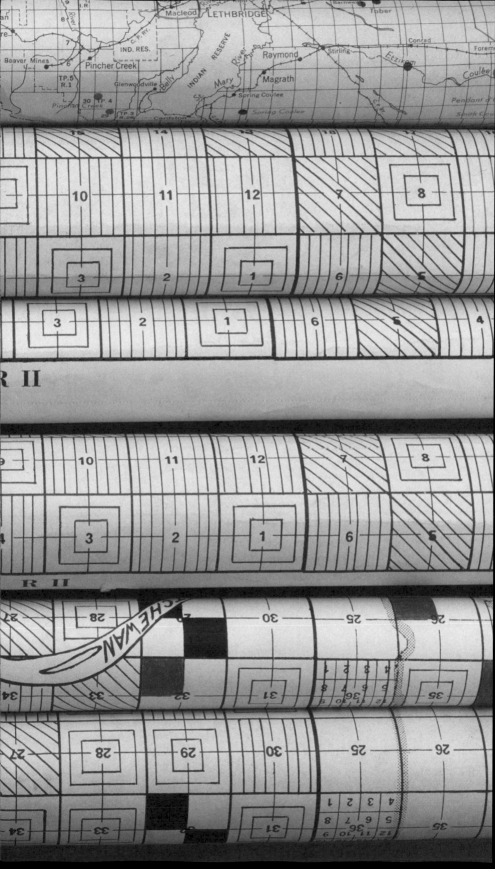

A Few Words to Scavengers

VANCOUVER

ALTHOUGH SCAVENGING IN FOREIGN LANDS IS a fascinating and absorbing travel pastime, there is nothing equal to rooting about in one's own hometown. Opportunities are best where familiarity with the locale leads the scavenger to the richest hoards of castoffs and where regular rounds are rewarded with a variety of loot. Also to be considered is the ease of getting one's finds home.[1]

Having to take airplanes—and worse, to cross borders—is a severe limitation for scavengers. Practiced as I am in tossing nonessentials from my luggage to accommodate precious finds,[2] I have been able to bring back an array of diverse items literally found on the streets of foreign cities. From Paris, I've hauled 45s of Indian music, lace, television wiring diagrams, and *cartes-cabinet;* from Aleppo, arithmetic primers in Arabic, travel documents in Turkish, and package labels in French. From Catania, I have brought game boards; from Tangier, playing cards; from London, sheet music; from Cairo, cigarette packages; from just about everywhere, subway and bus tickets. Among the many things I've found, I've left behind a portfolio folder (with a powerful musty odor), an old suitcase (after the discovery of a colony of silverfish), a television set (the source of the wiring diagram mentioned above), and a passport (turned in).

PREVIOUS SPREAD: *These maps, contained in a large, unwieldy case, would have been impossible to transport on a plane. Since they were found locally, however, they now have a place in my home.* ABOVE: *This rubber-stamp holder has been transformed into wall art.* FACING PAGE: *Wooden boxes, no matter how beat up, must always be rescued.*

---

1 This is a good place to make it clear that by "castoff," I do not mean anything that is not tied down. It is an object that has clearly been discarded.

2 Nonessentials are items like T-shirts, socks, sweaters, shampoo—in other words, anything without a negotiable value. I have been told of a woman who jettisoned the entire contents of her pack to squeeze in a scavenged billboard poster from Greece. I hope this is a true story.

The rusty cover plate to a streetlamp standard, all that was left when the post was replaced, became a frame for a small contact-print portrait.

As a place for finding beguiling trash, Vancouver may not be the best city in the world—superficially, at least, there is too much emphasis on the new and the disposable—but Vancouver is my hometown, and I've come to know its possibilities. Scavengers such as I stop short of purposely visiting the local landfills (we don't object to snooping around if we go there to drop something off, however), and we would never join the parade of back-alley bottle hunters, also known as dumpster divers. The magic of scavenging is in the serendipity of the find; to actually hunt for objects—though sometimes necessary—diminishes the pleasure of finding them.

Tables and chairs, carpets, posters, gardening tools, planters, curtain rods, even a hardhat, set out curbside with a "Free" sign following a garage sale, are a few of my finds. Some items fail inspection and either go straight to my curb or get rehabilitated or passed along to a charity shop. Others become part of that inventory of things I hope we all have that are impossible to part with.

Plummy residential neighborhoods are good for usable items: patio furniture, light fixtures, appliances; the downtown alleys are best for photogenic or curious objects. Because I spend more time in the city center, much of what I've come across in Vancouver has been moldy, disintegrating, odoriferous, or vermin infested—just the sort of thing I am not allowed to bring home. So I've settled for photographs of them. The relatively pristine figurine opposite was found *in situ* on a window sill in a back alley at Main and Hastings in the Downtown Eastside. A nearby, recent fire had only blackened portions of the brick of the building that harbored it. Under the circumstances, the figurine seemed positively talismanic and had to be left untouched.

Acknowledgments

I'm grateful to all the antique, collectible, and secondhand dealers I have ever had the pleasure to do business with. I would especially like to thank the following friends: Joan Story, who not only has shared many travel adventures but, most recently, has helped my memory along; Marv Newland, whose fine example taught me the importance of the travel journal; Nancy Flight, my editor, who kept her face free of the bewilderment she must have felt as she followed the evolution of this book; Mary Schendlinger, for her thorough copyediting; Iva Cheung, for her excellent proofreading; Marcia Moore, whose eclectic tastes are an education in seeing, and who tenaciously found, collected, and transported the Long Beach watercolor box for me; Rose Kish and Violet Smythe, for the help with Hungarian; Susan Kelso, for the Helmar cigarette package; Laurent Budik, an enthusiastic source of the unusual; and Todd Belcher, for the invaluable help with the photography. Special thanks to David Gay, my constant flea-market and travel companion.

Bibliography

Balzac, Honoré de. *Cousin Pons*. Translated by Herbert J. Hunt. Harmondsworth: Penguin, 1968 (first published in French, 1848).
———. *The Wild Ass's Skin*. Translated by Herbert J. Hunt. Harmondsworth: Penguin, 1977 (first published as *La Peau de chagrin*, 1831).

Barzini, Luigi. *The Italians*. New York: Atheneum, 1964.

Bertillon, Alphonse. *Instructions for Taking Descriptions for the Identification of Criminals and Others by the means of Anthropometric Indications*. Translated by Gallus Muller. Chicago: American Bertillon Prison Bureau, 1889.

Gosse, Edmund. "Pierre Loti" (1902), in *French Profiles*. London: William Heineman, 1913.

Harris, Walter. *Morocco That Was*. Edinburgh: William Blackwood, 1921.

von Sternberg, Josef. *Fun in a Chinese Laundry*. New York: Macmillan, 1965.

Index

...io ad Litem Evocare; Quia per Doctorem
cessuales, et ę Evictore factus est Possess
Actionem respondere non tenetur. U. J.
ense 1748.

8° Quamvis in Testibus super Citat
ratos Tabula, vel Judices Cottenses expe
hibitionem medio jurisdictioni eorundem
se, nisi tamen in specifico Nomina Jurisd
inserta sint Citatio condescendit; Si ille
medio Jurisdictionatorum fiant, quatenu
queat. Jam vero, si nomina eorum ex
dispositioni Legis satisfactum sit: Sufficient
is, medio cujus Citatio facta exponitur,
potest. U. J. in Caa Maria Juv=Vas

9° Si in una Possione plures si
Pagensis, vel Decurionis, qui tamen alter
tio condescendere solet; Quia Citatio
autem vel Vai Decuria tametsi quoad